Bond
No.1 for exam success

English Vocabulary

10 Minute Tests

CEM (Durham University)

10–11+ years

OXFORD
UNIVERSITY PRESS

OXFORD
UNIVERSITY PRESS

Great Clarendon Street, Oxford, OX2 6DP, United Kingdom

Oxford University Press is a department of the University of Oxford.
It furthers the University's objective of excellence in research,
scholarship, and education by publishing worldwide. Oxford
is a registered trade mark of Oxford University Press in the UK
and in certain other countries

Text © Oxford University Press 2018

Author: Christine Jenkins

The moral rights of the author have been asserted

First published in 2018

All rights reserved. No part of this publication may be reproduced,
stored in a retrieval system, or transmitted, in any form or by any
means, without the prior permission in writing of Oxford University
Press, or as expressly permitted by law, by licence or under terms
agreed with the appropriate reprographics rights organization.
Enquiries concerning reproduction outside the scope of the above
should be sent to the Rights Department, Oxford University Press,
at the address above.

You must not circulate this work in any other form and you must
impose this same condition on any acquirer

British Library Cataloguing in Publication Data
Data available

978-0-19-276766-0

10 9 8 7 6 5

Paper used in the production of this book is a natural, recyclable
product made from wood grown in sustainable forests.
The manufacturing process conforms to the environmental
regulations of the country of origin.

Printed in the United Kingdom

Acknowledgements

Cover illustration: Lo Cole
Illustrations: Aptara
Page make-up: Aptara

Useful notes

These 10-minute tests will help you develop your vocabulary, understand challenging words in context and learn a wide range of synonyms and antonyms. Developing a wide vocabulary is useful when doing 11+ tests, and it will also help you improve your reading, writing and spoken language skills. The tests are designed to challenge you and to encourage you to think and work quickly.

There is a variety of question formats, with different numbers and types of questions per section. Sometimes you will have a space to fill in missing letters or words, while other questions are multiple choice. In some questions, you will be given a grid of words or definitions to match. Make sure to read the instructions carefully each time. Always choose the best possible answer from any options given.

Use a dictionary and thesaurus to look up unknown words. Write down any new words, their definitions and any synonyms and antonyms. Keep looking through your words and, when you feel confident, try using them: say them in sentences and write them in your school work or on a whiteboard. Create a word-search puzzle or ask someone to test you on the meanings. When you read a book or website, paying attention to any unknown words will help to extend your vocabulary too.

Try making flashcards of any unknown words. Write a word on one side of the card, with as many synonyms as you can find in the thesaurus. You can write the antonyms on the back of the card and then test yourself. Another idea is to write one word on the front of a card and one synonym on the front of another card. You can then match the synonyms.

As you work through the book, highlight any questions that you find difficult. Ask yourself if it is the particular style of question you find tricky, or whether there were certain words that you did not know. You could jot them down and learn them after checking the answers.

The Progress Chart on page 96 is a great way of visualising your progress, and the puzzles are fun activities that will help extend and consolidate word skills. The Answers pages give explanations as to why the answer given is correct and, sometimes, why the other options are incorrect.

Keep consolidating the new words you have learnt, but remember that no exam expects you to know every word or to score 100% in everything. Learning new vocabulary needs to remain an activity that helps you to explore the richness of words that you can use in your own writing and to help you develop your comprehension skills.

Test 1

Select the **ONE** word on the right that has the most **SIMILAR** meaning to the word on the left. Underline the correct answer.

1 abundant   **a** juicy   **b** plenteous   **c** inadequate   **d** scarce   **e** supply

2 avid   **a** smart   **b** special   **c** hard-working   **d** eager   **e** apathetic

3 component   **a** element   **b** side   **c** composition   **d** compliment   **e** addition

4 diplomatic   **a** severe   **b** official   **c** royal   **d** tactful   **e** rude

5 cumbersome   **a** tiny   **b** cold   **c** tall   **d** bulky   **e** extra

The following sentences all have **ONE** word missing. Complete each sentence by selecting the **BEST** word from options **a–e**. Underline the correct answer.

6 The journalist wrote an _____ about a spate of burglaries in the area.

   a newspaper   **b** magazine   **c** article   **d** extra   **e** feature

7 Martha _____ her hair last week, but did not like the colour.

   a died   **b** dead   **c** colours   **d** dye   **e** dyed

8 Every Friday morning, the fire alarms were _____.

   a rang   **b** rings   **c** testing   **d** tested   **e** ringed

9 The quiz team _____ quietly about the answer before they wrote it down.

   a conditioned   **b** conferred   **c** consisted   **d** prompted   **e** participated

10 The house had been _____ for five years.

   a immobile   **b** ruined   **c** unoccupied   **d** barren   **e** discarded

Complete the word on the right so that it has the most **OPPOSITE** meaning to the word on the left.

11 voluntary   o _ l _ _ t _ _ y

12 impulsive   d e _ _ b _ _ _ _

13 uncouth   _ o _ _ t e

14 fair   b _ _ _ e d

15 conceal   e _ _ o s _

Vocabulary Tip!

When looking for the antonyms or synonyms of words, consider whether the word given has more than one meaning. Think about each meaning when finding the correct answer.

Read the following sentence and answer the questions. Underline the most sensible word from options **a–d**.

'In her capacity as Mayor, Councillor Stevens pronounced the new leisure complex open.'

16 What does the word 'capacity' mean in this sentence?

   a ability   b engagement   c space   d role

17 What does the word 'pronounced' mean in this sentence?

   a declared   b opened   c accented   d stressed

18 What does the word 'complex' mean in this sentence?

   a complicated   b complete   c pool   d facility

Test 2

Test time: 0 — 5 — 10 minutes

The following sentences all have **ONE** word missing. Complete each sentence by selecting the **BEST** word from options **a–e**. Underline the correct answer.

1 Dad decided to _____ his lifetime ambition to run a marathon.

   a enter   b fulfil   c succeed   d train   e end

2 Despite the rain, the race went _____.

   a forwards   b over   c across   d continued   e ahead

3 Emily had been learning to drive _____ a fortnight.

   a since   b whilst   c every   d for   e only

4 The artist had a range of materials _____ his disposal.

   a at   b for   c on   d in   e to

Find the three-letter word that is needed to complete each word so that each sentence makes sense. Underline the **TWO** answers needed from options **a–e**.

5 The _____inesswoman checked her em_____s regularly.

   a son   b ail   c bus   d men   e sun

6 The choir pr_____ised every Wednesday in the commu_____y centre.

   a nut   b rat   c art   d act   e nit

7 Michael made a large _____r in his jeans when he sc_____bled over the gate.

   a rip   b ram   c rum   d tea   e pea

> **Time-saving Tip!**
> You don't have time to write out all possible combinations for these question types, but if you are struggling to decide between one or two options, writing the word out in your own handwriting really helps.

Find the missing **THREE** letters that complete these words. The three letters do not have to make a word. The same three letters are used for both words.

8   fati_____   ton_____

9   ho_____on   p_____e

10 l_____er   _____enious

11 _____lify   e_____l

> **Letter Tip!**
> Use your knowledge of letter combinations to help with these questions. You could also try covering up the word with your finger and then slowly reveal part of the word, forwards or backwards. This can make it easier to predict the word or to generate other words that might be related.

Read the following paragraph and add **ONE** word from the list to each space so that the paragraph makes sense. There are more words than there are spaces so some will be left out, but each word can only be used once.

eats   were   knew   looking   stare   would   was   ate   thinking

12–16 The children _____ their lunch

contentedly, _____ out of the windows

and _____ of the mountains there

_____ be to climb, the ponds, the streams to fish, the

pictures to take, and the stories they _____ to hear all

summer long.

Time for a break! ★ Go to Puzzle Page 84 →

Test 3

Find the three-letter word that is needed to complete each word so that each sentence makes sense. The same three letters are used for both words. Underline the answer needed from options **a–e**.

1. With a fl_____ish, the j_____nalist left the room angrily.

   a air   **b** ill   **c** aim   **d** err   **e** our

2. Anyone who did not a_____e by the rules was for_____den from taking part.

   a bud   **b** ten   **c** bid   **d** bad   **e** pea

3. I _____d him money for the fl_____ers.

   a ten   **b** end   **c** our   **d** out   **e** owe

4. There was a staff brie_____g to discuss school _____ances.

   a sun   **b** fin   **c** din   **d** fan   **e** den

5. The _____didate had found the job va_____cy advertised online.

   a cut   **b** con   **c** ant   **d** can   **e** ran

Select the **TWO** odd words out on each line. Select your answers by underlining **TWO** of the options **a–e**.

6. **a** deluge   **b** pipe   **c** torrent   **d** downpour   **e** soaking

7. **a** peaceful   **b** muted   **c** noise   **d** silence   **e** hushed

8. **a** satchel   **b** carry   **c** kit   **d** bag   **e** briefcase

The following sentences all have **ONE** word missing. Complete each sentence by selecting the **BEST** word from options **a–e**. Underline the correct answer.

9   Jamal _____ he should have revised earlier.

   a wished   **b** knew   **c** new   **d** think   **e** know

10 She decided to go out _____ the spur of the moment.

   a in   **b** an   **c** for   **d** at   **e** on

11 I went to football _____ every Friday.

   a match   **b** stadium   **c** practise   **d** practice   **e** practising

12 The weeds in the courtyard were _____ of control.

   a out   **b** under   **c** overgrown   **d** often   **e** in

13 The dancer continued with the show _____ hurting his ankle.

   a when   **b** although   **c** because   **d** despite   **e** whilst

> **'Best' Answer Tip!**
>
> When a question asks for the 'best' answer, there are often other options that *could* fit. Read the sentence through a few times to help you decide which one word or phrase sounds the best and makes the most sense in the context of the sentence.

Select the **ONE** word on the right that has the most **SIMILAR** meaning to the word on the left. Underline the correct answer.

14 decayed   **a** damp   **b** rotten   **c** bad   **d** smelly   **e** mould

15 excuse   **a** sorry   **b** spoil   **c** commit   **d** punish   **e** absolve

16 listless   **a** disorganised   **b** sad   **c** wonky   **d** lethargic   **e** silly

Test 4

Complete the word on the right so that it has the most **OPPOSITE** meaning to the word on the left.

1. distinct — v _ _ u _

2. significant — _ r _ v _ _ l

3. luxurious — f _ _ _ a l

4. methodical — c _ a _ t _ _

5. improve — w _ r _ _ n

6. imprisonment — l _ _ e _ t _

Find the **THREE** letters needed to complete each word so that each sentence makes sense. Underline the answer needed from options **a–e**.

7. The choir rehea_____d every Wednesday for the concert.

   a ear   **b** rea   **c** rse   **d** eer   **e** sse

8. Carmel came second in the di_____ict swimming competition.

   a str   **b** cst   **c** sst   **d** tri   **e** ssi

9. The driver had to swerve to avoid a c_____ision.

   a olo   **b** ool   **c** oll   **d** ell   **e** ill

Underline the correct word in each of these sentences.

10 Being hit by a football left her in a (days / **daze**).

11 The chocolate cake had a very (**dense** / dents), moist texture.

12 The surveyor found woodworm in the (eves / **eaves**) of the house.

13 The cut on her foot (heeled / **healed**) quickly.

14 The trousers had a high (**waist** / waste).

> *Homophone Tip!*
> If you are unsure which of the two words is the correct one, look for related words. Thinking about the meaning of those can help you to decide which is correct. For example, in the sentence 'The vet wanted to find the dog's weight / wait', 'weight' contains the word 'weigh'.

The following sentences all have **ONE** word missing. Complete each sentence by selecting the **BEST** word from options **a–e**. Underline the correct answer.

15 The tightrope had to be _____ in order to hold the acrobat.

    a taught   **b** fraught   **c** tensing   **d** taut   **e** tied

16 The children all had to learn a poem to _____.

    a recede   **b** resite   **c** recent   **d** insight   **e** recite

17 The actor needed prompting when she missed her _____.

    a cue   **b** code   **c** queue   **d** play   **e** quote

Time for a break! ★ Go to Puzzle Page 85 →

Test 5

Complete the word on the right so that it has the **SAME** or **SIMILAR** meaning to the word on the left.

1. quickly — h u r _ _ d _ y
2. robust — s _ _ r _ _
3. curb — r _ s _ r a _ _
4. interfering — i _ t _ u _ _ e
5. rival — a _ _ _ r _ a _ y
6. divert — d _ f _ _ t

Read the following paragraph and add **ONE** word from the list to each space so that the paragraph makes sense. There are more words than there are spaces so some will be left out, but each word can only be used once.

> rehearsals   stage   orchestra   curtain   performance
> excitement   show   theatre

7–12 Jemima read through her lines one last time. She could hear the _____ playing the overture and she knew that the _____ would rise at any moment. A tingle of nerves and _____ rushed through her body. After weeks of _____, she knew she was ready. Hoping to give her best _____ ever, she stepped onto the _____.

Select the **ONE** word on the right that has the most **OPPOSITE** meaning to the word on the left. Underline the correct answer.

13 advance   **a** recent   **b** retreat   **c** retrain   **d** ahead   **e** backwards

14 risky   **a** safely   **b** harmful   **c** safe   **d** steadily   **e** danger

15 blunt   **a** cut   **b** tight   **c** dull   **d** knife   **e** sharp

16 better   **a** bad   **b** worst   **c** worse   **d** improve   **e** awful

17 identical **a** same   **b** similar   **c** indifferent   **d** difference   **e** different

18 chaotic   **a** messy   **b** orderly   **c** shiny   **d** clean   **e** tidily

> **Word Tip!**
> Always think about which word class the given word is. The antonym you choose must be the same. For example, 'hot' is an adjective, so its antonym ('cold') would also be an adjective.

Underline the **ONE** word from the brackets on the left and the **ONE** word from those on the right that have the most **SIMILAR** meanings.

19 (sumptuous   immense   barren)   (tall   weary   extravagant)

20 (savage   anxiety   peril)   (enjoyment   hazard   truth)

21 (affectionate   determined   swift)   (total   swollen   abrupt)

22 (combination   competition   commendation)   (contest   sequel   event)

Test 6

Look at the words in the grid and then use them to answer the questions that follow.

a	frequent	b	substantial	c	sad	d	melancholy	e	special
f	empty	g	small	h	rude	i	immense	j	impudent
k	bent	l	affluent	m	twisted	n	tight	o	kind
p	sorrow	q	straight	r	happy	s	wealthy	t	respectful

1 Find **TWO** synonyms for 'crooked'.
   _____   _____

2 Find **TWO** synonyms for 'big'.
   _____   _____

3 Find **TWO** antonyms for 'poor'.
   _____   _____

4 Find **TWO** antonyms for 'polite'.
   _____   _____

5 Find **TWO** synonyms for 'sadness'.
   _____   _____

Select the **TWO** odd words out on each line. Select your answers by underlining **TWO** of the options **a–e**.

6 a needless   b useful   c vital   d unnecessary   e pointless

7 a rowdy   b placid   c boisterous   d lazy   e raucous

8 a spanner   b hammer   c tool   d fix   e screwdriver

Underline the correct word in each of these sentences.

9 As part of her stable duties, Gemma groomed the horse's (mane / main).

10 The vintage uniform was embellished in an elaborate (manor / manner).

11 A trip to the city made everyone appreciate the clean (air / heir) of the countryside.

12 Driving down a country lane, Noel was forced to stop when a (heard / herd) of cows crossed the road.

13 The nurse tried in (vane / vein / vain) to calm the patient down.

Read the following sentences and answer the questions. Underline the most sensible word from options **a–d**.

'The headteacher addressed the pupils and parents to inform them about the imminent changes to the examination arrangements.'

14 What does the word 'addressed' mean in this sentence?

   a presented   **b** called   **c** spoke to   **d** wrote

15 What does the word 'inform' mean in this sentence?

   a ask   **b** betray   **c** remind   **d** notify

16 What does the word 'imminent' mean in this sentence?

   a forthcoming   **b** important   **c** extra   **d** recent

'He advised them that older siblings had been tested under a different system.'

17 What does the word 'siblings' mean in this sentence?

   a relatives   **b** children   **c** brothers and sisters   **d** acquaintances

Test 7

Find the three-letter word that is needed to complete each word so that each sentence makes sense. Underline the **TWO** answers needed from options **a–e**.

1 Chris _____ed having his p_____o taken.

   a hot   **b** hit   **c** hat   **d** het   **e** not

2 The audience burst into r_____urous appla_____ at the end of the show.

   a art   **b** opt   **c** use   **d** apt   **e** ace

3 Jessica broke her t_____b playing hoc_____.

   a ham   **b** hum   **c** coy   **d** key   **e** hay

4 The opera singer had grown a bu_____ b_____d especially for the role.

   a she   **b** ear   **c** air   **d** shy   **e** ray

5 Nadia sat the ad_____ced _____hs exam.

   a met   **b** mum   **c** van   **d** vat   **e** mat

Underline the correct word in each of these sentences.

6 Ashes from the fire fell into the (great / grate).

7 When she lifted the rock, the soil below was (teeming / teaming) with insects.

8 The (cellar / seller) was full of new products ready for the market.

9 The Queen kept her (hoarse / horse) on a very tight (rein / reign / rain).

10 As she (passed / past) the window, she noticed her friend inside.

Read the following paragraph and add **ONE** word from the list to each space so that the paragraph makes sense. There are more words than there are spaces so some will be left out, but each word can only be used once.

| presenting | hear | surprise | here | formal | realised | former |

11–15 Sitting in her car in the traffic jam, Tiana suddenly _____ that she knew the voice on the radio. It was her _____ English teacher, Mr Martin, who had taught her about Shakespeare many years ago. Now _____ he was, _____ a show about the plays. What a _____!

Match each word on the left to the word with the **OPPOSITE** meaning on the right by drawing a line.

16 indolent   lead

17 follow   industrious

18 frail   permit

19 prohibit   discouraged

20 undaunted   certain

21 doubtful   strong

Test 8

Select the **ONE** word on the right that has the most **SIMILAR** meaning to the word on the left. Underline the correct answer.

1 savour   a appreciate   b salty   c tasty   d eat   e wish

2 bemused   a dangerous   b silly   c confused   d sensible   e belittled

3 dismal   a gloomy   b lonely   c unreliable d lazy   e distant

4 flamboyant a wealthy   b extravagant c pretty   d ugly   e feathery

5 obscure   a dirty   b even   c bad   d unclear   e open

Find the missing three-letter word that completes these words. The same three letters are used for both words.

6 va_____t   _____cel

7 ca_____al   hos_____al

8 ch_____   _____tight

9 sp_____t   t_____et

10 gua_____tee   frag_____ce

11 in_____mation   _____bidden

Spelling Tip!

Look for common letter combinations before and after the letters you need to find. For example, in one word there is a 'c' followed by an 'h'. Is the next letter likely to be a vowel if two consonants are given next to each other?

Look at the words in the grid and then use them to answer the questions that follow.

a	unsuccessful	b	desert	c	blank	d	dirty	e	outer
f	exterior	g	fortunate	h	coarse	i	inside	j	dinner
k	observer	l	creature	m	cores	n	fortuitous	o	mess
p	total	q	occupied	r	dessert	s	person	t	course

12 Find **TWO** antonyms for 'interior'.

_____   _____

13 Find **ONE** word that means the same as the phrase 'fly on the wall'.

_____

14 Find **ONE** word that means the same as 'rough'.

_____

15 Find **ONE** word that means 'to abandon someone'.

_____

16 Find **ONE** word that means the same as 'pudding'.

_____

17 Find **TWO** antonyms for 'unlucky'.

_____   _____

Vocabulary Grid Tip!
Remember that some words have more than one meaning. As you look through the words in the grid, try to think how many meanings of the word there are.

Test 9

Select the **TWO** odd words out on each line. Select your answers by underlining **TWO** of the options **a–e**.

1 **a** seagull   **b** snail   **c** crow   **d** fox   **e** lark

2 **a** table   **b** spoon   **c** plate   **d** knife   **e** fork

3 **a** brook   **b** river   **c** stream   **d** reservoir   **e** pond

4 **a** pear   **b** carrot   **c** potato   **d** crop   **e** parsnip

5 **a** forest   **b** leaf   **c** grow   **d** twig   **e** branch

Odd One Out Tip!
Think of ways of grouping words: for example, are some of them different types of the same thing? Look for what they do or how they are used.

Complete the word on the right so that it has the **SAME** or **SIMILAR** meaning to the word on the left.

6 worried | a | n | | | | |

7 dwelling | r | e | | | e | | c | |

8 sly | | | n | | | n | g |

9 begin | c | | m | | | | |

10 smell | | d | | | r |

Select the **ONE** word on the right that has the most **OPPOSITE** meaning to the word on the left. Underline the correct answer.

11 despair   a decline   b ruin   c hope   d worry   e contempt

12 flexible   a strong   b robust   c bendy   d capable   e rigid

13 brief   a lengthy   b short   c tight   d quick   e stern

14 often   a regularly b soon   c seldom   d frequently e certainly

15 distinct   a clear   b vague   c special   d pretty   e total

16 cheap   a economical b wealthy   c money   d poverty   e costly

Underline the correct phrase in each of these sentences.

17 (The least / At least) the weather had improved by the time the fair opened.

18 It was (by no means / in no means) certain that she would get a position on the football team.

19 The exact arrangements for the forthcoming summer festival were still (under suspicion / under discussion).

20 The organisers offered a discount on tickets bought (on advance / in advance).

21 Her long-lost cousin contacted her (out of the blue / in the red).

Test 10

Find the missing letters that complete the word on the right so that it has a **SIMILAR** meaning to the word on the left. Underline the correct answer from options **a–e**.

1 calm   t __ a __ __ u i __

   a rqui   **b** anql   **c** rnql   **d** ranq   **e** rlql

2 strange   p __ __ u __ i __ r

   a reca   **b** ecla   **c** ecle   **d** ekla   **e** arle

3 heroic   v __ __ i __ n __

   a alet   **b** alad   **c** ilat   **d** alat   **e** atlt

4 idle   in __ c __ i __ __

   a atve   **b** acve   **c** lcte   **d** actv   **e** evte

---

Match each word on the left to the word with the most **OPPOSITE** meaning on the right by drawing a line.

5   prosperous   boastful

6   vast   impoverished

7   punctual   ally

8   foe   remove

9   humble   loyalty

10 betrayal   tardy

11 insert   restricted

The following sentences all have **ONE** word missing. Complete each sentence by selecting the **BEST** word from options **a–e**. Underline the correct answer.

12 The prize was donated by a _____ local businesswoman.

    a preposterous   **b** amazing   **c** affluent   **d** prominent   **e** probable

13 In Victorian times, wealthy families often employed _____ servants.

    a majestic   **b** prosperous   **c** interesting   **d** pathetic   **e** domestic

14 Emil had to _____ an application for the role of children's playleader.

    a substitute   **b** resign   **c** submerge   **d** commit   **e** submit

15 The Grimshaw family invited their new neighbours in, to become better _____.

    a offended   **b** obliged   **c** perceived   **d** acquainted   **e** experienced

16 The safety inspector explained that the _____ of his visit was to check the play equipment.

    a attempt   **b** purpose   **c** consideration   **d** assistance   **e** security

---

Complete the word on the right so that it has the most **OPPOSITE** meaning to the word on the left.

17 greed   g _ _ e r _ s t y

18 insult   f _ a _ _ e _

19 extend   a b _ r _ v i a _ _

20 sullen   _ h _ e r _ u _

Test 11

Find the missing three-letter word that completes these words. The same three letters are used for both words.

1 am_____ion   _____ter

2 just_____   magnif_____nt

3 harb_____   fl_____ish

4 c_____it   inspi_____

5 ex_____sive   sus_____d

6 c_____idate   ab_____on

Read the following sentences and answer the questions. Underline the most sensible word from options **a–e**.

'The butcher sold meat and poultry.'

7 What does the word 'poultry' mean in this sentence?

   a groceries   **b** vegetarian food   **c** fish   **d** vegetables   **e** fowl

'Everyone was invited to contribute towards a retirement present for Mrs Jones.'

8 What does the word 'contribute' mean in this sentence?

   a find   **b** donate   **c** collect   **d** count   **e** buy

'Chaya seldom wrote letters home but she kept in touch by text.'

9 What does the word 'seldom' mean in this sentence?

   a often   **b** usually   **c** only   **d** rarely   **e** never

Select the **TWO** odd words out on each line. Select your answers by underlining **TWO** of the options **a–e**.

10   a haughty   b lofty   c happy   d disdainful   e naughty

11   a jug   b pint   c gallon   d water   e litre

12   a conundrum   b worried   c difficult   d dilemma   e problem

13   a limit   b restrict   c pass   d grow   e curb

Read the following paragraph and add **ONE** word from the list to each space so that the paragraph makes sense. There are more words than there are spaces so some will be left out, but each word can only be used once.

bored   board   exhaustion   luggage   harbour   excitement   vessel   wave

14–19   The _____ had been at sea for many weeks

and the passengers on _____ were weary and

_____. As the _____

finally came into sight, their _____ turned into

_____ upon realising the opportunities ahead of them.

Choosing Words Tip!
Always read the passage through first to get a sense of what it is about. This helps you to decide which words make the most sense in the context. When you have made your choices, read it through again.

Test 12

Find the missing three-letter word that completes these words so that the sentence makes sense. Write the three-letter word in the grid on the right-hand side.

1 Maya's mum asked her to run an er_____d.

2 The couple paid a depo_____ for their holiday.

3 It took two years for the business to make a pro_____.

4 The cook had to esti_____e how many meals would be con_____ed each week.

5 Dad made sure he took plenty of games to oc_____y the children on their j_____ney.

Look at the words in the grid and then use them to answer the questions that follow.

a	tall	b	conceited	c	free	d	open	e	solid
f	full	g	harsh	h	pale	i	allow	j	run
k	wander	l	boastful	m	stern	n	modern	o	roam
p	holy	q	release	r	accept	s	nervous	t	lonely

6 Find **TWO** antonyms for 'refuse'.

7 Find **TWO** antonyms for 'hollow'.

8 Find **TWO** antonyms for 'modest'.

9 Find **TWO** antonyms for 'restrain'.

_____   _____

10 Find **TWO** synonyms for 'ramble'.

_____   _____

11 Find **TWO** synonyms for 'severe'.

_____   _____

Read the following sentences and answer the questions. Underline the most sensible answer from options **a–d**.

'It was important to immerse the T-shirt in the dye.'

12 What does the word 'immerse' mean in this sentence?

a rub   **b** submerge   **c** paint   **d** wash

'The coastguard was notified that the canoeists were in peril.'

13 What does the word 'notified' mean in this sentence?

a prepared   **b** recorded   **c** telephoned   **d** informed

14 What does the phrase 'in peril' mean in this sentence?

a informed   **b** inexperienced   **c** in the water   **d** in danger

'When we move, our muscles contract.'

15 What does the word 'contract' mean in this sentence?

a promise   **b** expand   **c** tighten   **d** relax

Gemma studied Ryan's face to see if he was in earnest.

16 What does the phrase 'in earnest' mean in this sentence?

a in danger   **b** elderly   **c** incapable   **d** serious

Test 13

Read the following paragraph and add **ONE** word from the list to each space so that the paragraph makes sense. There are more words than there are spaces so some will be left out, but each word can only be used once.

> provoke   absurd   restrained   entirely   attempt   moderate
> peculiar   refused

1–6 It was alien dress-up day at school and Josh had decided to wear the

most _____ costume he could make, in an

_____ to _____ a reaction.

He _____ to listen to his mum when she told him how

_____ he looked dressed _____ in

silver foil and metal coat hangers!

Missing Words Tip!
There may be more than one word that fits, but there will always be one that makes better sense in the context of the whole passage. Don't try to be creative in this kind of exercise: it is all about understanding the vocabulary!

Complete the word on the right so that it has a **SIMILAR** meaning to the word on the left.

7 sleek | s | o | | h |

8 expel | b | | i | h |

9 prosper | f | o | | r | i | s |

Complete the word on the right so that it has the **OPPOSITE** meaning to the word on the left.

10 fertile   b _ _ _ e n

11 commonplace   _ _ _ e _

12 unite   _ _ v i _ e

Select the **TWO** odd words out on each line. Select your answers by underlining **TWO** of the options **a–e**.

13 a scarf   b mackintosh   c anorak   d overcoat   e glove

14 a millennium b decade   c fortnight d century   e day

15 a linger   b loiter   c dawdle   d continue   e hurry

16 a merchant   b profit   c buy   d trader   e dealer

Underline the **ONE** word from the brackets on the left and the **ONE** word from those on the right that have the most **SIMILAR** meaning.

17 (crowd   concert   space)   (party   throng   noisy)

18 (foundation   ambition   condition)   (aspiration   tuition   reaction)

19 (fecund   exhausted   objectionable)   (complimentary   rough   fertile)

Time for a break! ★ Go to Puzzle Page 88 →

Test 14

Match each word on the left to the word with a **SIMILAR** meaning on the right by drawing a line.

1   economical   deceive

2   decline   whimsical

3   trick   coax

4   quaint   prudent

5   entice   denounce

6   condemn   deteriorate

Underline the correct word in each of these sentences.

7   All students were expected to conform (to / about / by) the uniform rules.

8   In spite (at / to / of) the weather, they continued to climb to the summit.

9   It is difficult to untie your shoelaces (so / when / with) your hands are cold.

10 According (on / by / to) the website, the offer ended at midnight.

11 The receptionist phoned Mrs Newton (on / in / by) behalf (at / with / of) the doctor.

Find the missing three-letter word that completes these words. The same three letters are used for both words.

12 mul_____le   _____toe

13 _____istic   dep_____

14 as_____e   con_____er

15 desc_____e   sc_____ble

Read the following sentences and answer the questions. Underline the most sensible word from options **a–d**.

'The teaching assistant tried to resolve the conflict between the two pupils.'

16 What does the word 'resolve' mean in this sentence?

   a punish   **b** supervise   **c** settle   **d** inflict

'After 31 October, all business at the company would cease.'

17 What does the word 'cease' mean in this sentence?

   a stop   **b** profit   **c** remove   **d** continue

'"We don't want any broken limbs!" shouted the gym instructor.'

18 What does the word 'limbs' mean in this sentence?

   a legs   **b** bones   **c** feet and hands   **d** arms and legs

19 What does the word 'instructor' mean in this sentence?

   a someone who reads instructions   **b** a professional athlete
   c a teacher or coach   **d** a volunteer

Test 15

Select the **ONE** word on the right that has the most **OPPOSITE** meaning to the word on the left. Underline the correct answer.

1 deny   a decline   b punish   c hope   d admit   e obey

2 restore   a build   b broken   c destroy   d open   e deactivate

3 concentrated   a serious   b tight   c rich   d fragile   e diluted

4 prompt   a punctual   b tardy   c efficient   d moderate   e vacant

5 sincere   a earnest   b blunt   c perilous   d devout   e flippant

Vocabulary Tip!

When looking for antonyms, try using the given word in a sentence. Then replace it with each of the options. The word you select to replace it with should change the meaning of the sentence without making any other changes.

Match each word on the left to the word with the most **OPPOSITE** meaning on the right by drawing a line.

6 arduous   unsanitary

7 benevolent   effortless

8 unkempt   mean

9 hygienic   neat

Select the **TWO** odd words out on each line. Select your answers by underlining **TWO** of the options **a–e**.

10   **a** modest   **b** arrogant   **c** humble   **d** unassuming   **e** mortal

11   **a** remorseful   **b** angry   **c** repentant   **d** curious   **e** apologetic

12   **a** contempt   **b** quarrel   **c** dispute   **d** shout   **e** argument

13   **a** signature   **b** article   **c** promise   **d** oath   **e** pledge

14   **a** attempt   **b** avoid   **c** bid   **d** endeavour   **e** oppress

---

Find the missing **THREE** letters to complete these words so that the sentence makes sense. The three letters do not have to make a word. Write the three letters in the grid on the right-hand side.

15   The dry cleaners also offered a sewing service for any __ a __ m __ nts needing repair.

16   Living next to a busy road meant __ ons __ an __ traffic noise.

17   The t __ n __ n __ signed an __ gr __ eme __ t to rent the house for six months.

18   The police s __ __ z __ d the criminal's po __ se __ s __ ons.

Test 16

Find the missing letters that complete the word so that the sentence makes sense. Underline the correct answer from options **a–e**.

1 It was so snowy, he decided to a ___ ___ n ___ ___ n the car.

   a bura   **b** bado   **c** badu   **d** bran   **e** bada

2 The whole co ___ ___ u ___ i ___ y clubbed together to raise money.

   a mmnd   **b** umnt   **c** mmnt   **d** bbun   **e** mmut

3 The di___ a___ ___ d ___ ted van had broken down.

   a lpaa   **b** lpia   **c** plii   **d** lipd   **e** plad

4 She hoped that by sitting in the corner she would be in ___ on ___ ___ i ___ uous.

   a cspc   **b** cscs   **c** cpia   **d** cpto   **e** cspt

5 It was a ___ ui ___ a ___ ___ e when the council closed the road for repairs.

   a tsns   **b** ncnc   **c** nsec   **d** nsnc   **e** nsns

---

Underline the correct word or phrase in each of these sentences.

6 It was (out of / not a / never) the question to leave school early.

7 Sam was (at the / on the / in the) lookout for props to use in the pantomime.

8 They made it (before / out of / just in) time for the concert.

9 She was (fed up with / fed up by / fed by) her bossy sister.

Select the **ONE** word on the right that has the most **SIMILAR** meaning to the word on the left. Underline the correct answer.

10 stubborn   a blunt   b rude   c malicious   d stern   e obstinate

11 ostentatious   a awful   b modest   c extravagant   d awkward   e heavy

12 perplexed   a difficult   b bored   c fake   d baffled   e complicated

13 meagre   a ghostly   b nearby   c monstrous   d scant   e generous

14 chastise   a reprimand   b chase   c shout   d forgive   e spoil

> **Word Tip!**
> Sometimes you might have two words that seem equally good. Try thinking of a sentence using the given word. Then try the same sentence again, but this time, replace the word with the other words to see which is the *most* similar.

Underline the correct word in each of these sentences.

15 The lights came on when the (sensor / censor) was activated.

16 They had booked a cabin with two (births / berths) on the cruise.

17 It was the steward's job to (martial / marshal) the spectators into the arena.

18 The nurse struggled to find a (vein / vane / vain).

19 She continued her (ascent / accent / assent) of the mountain despite the bad weather conditions.

Time for a break! ★ *Go to Puzzle Page 89* →

Test 17

Read the following paragraph and add **ONE** word from the list to each space so that the paragraph makes sense. There are more words than there are spaces so some will be left out, but each word can only be used once.

avoid   intention   rural   urban   tranquillity   quenched   scenic   saw

1–6 It was a hot summer's day and the family had decided to go on a trip to the countryside. Mum suggested they _____ the motorway so instead they took the _____ route. Soon, they left the town behind them and were driving on more _____ roads. After an hour or so, they stopped to have a picnic. The cold cans of lemonade they had packed in the cool bag _____ their thirst. They had no _____ of leaving the peace and _____ of the field for some time.

Each of the following pairs of sentences has a missing word. The same word can be used to complete both sentences, although the meaning is different. Write the word in the boxes.

7 The accountant had worked for the _____ for 20 years.

Priya wanted some _____ as she had been on her own all day.

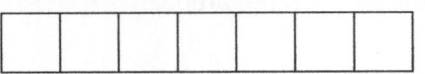

8 The criminal had obviously gone to _____.

The _____ was very slippery after the torrential rain.

9 Jeremy decided to _____ the new song he had written.

The Olympic medallist wanted to beat her previous _____.

[ ][ ][ ][ ][ ]

10 They moved out of their flat because they needed more _____.

In the future, it may be possible to travel to _____.

[ ][ ][ ][ ][ ]

11 Before baking the pie, the chef used a knife to _____ the top of the pastry.

His highest _____ was over 200.

[ ][ ][ ][ ][ ]

Look at the words in the grid and then use them to answer the questions that follow.

a	polite	b	gregarious	c	abrupt	d	rough	e	sluggish
f	accustom	g	significant	h	option	i	omen	j	prohibit
k	vague	l	seldom	m	vacant	n	retain	o	latter
p	companionable	q	offhand	r	agile	s	coax	t	sprightly

12 Find **TWO** synonyms for 'nimble'.

_____   _____

13 Find **TWO** synonyms for 'sociable'.

_____   _____

14 Find **TWO** antonyms for 'courteous'.

_____   _____

15 Find **ONE** word meaning 'an event that is perceived to be a bad sign of things to come'.

_____

Test 18

Underline the correct word in each of these sentences.

1. He had tickets for the top (tier / tear) of seats.

2. Mum chose a red scarf to (complement / compliment) her dress.

3. They were warned not to get off until the train was (stationery / stationary).

4. Mobile phones were not (aloud / allowed) in school.

5. The (sight / site) of the new school was inspected regularly.

> **Homophone Tip!**
> Try to find silly ways to memorise which word is which. For example, you 'h**ear**' with your '**ear**'. Draw silly cartoons to illustrate them or write the words with the important letters in different colours to help you learn them.

Match each word on the left to its definition on the right by drawing a line.

6. yield — land covered with grass

7. famine — a person who is greatly admired or worshipped

8. pioneer — land too poor to produce any vegetation

9. idol — a scarcity of food

10. pasture — the amount of a crop produced

11. barren — a person who is first to explore or discover something

Answers

Test 1 (pages 4–5)

1 b plenteous

The closest synonym to 'abundant' is 'plenteous', meaning plentiful in supply. 'Scarce' and 'inadequate' are antonyms of 'abundant'. 'Supply' and 'juicy' are incorrect, although sometimes used in phrases in connection with 'abundant'.

2 d eager

The closest synonym to 'avid' is 'eager', meaning keen. 'Smart', 'special' and 'hard-working' may be related qualities, but are not synonyms. 'Apathetic' is an antonym of 'avid'.

3 a element

The closest synonym to 'component' is 'element', meaning a constituent part.

4 d tactful

The closest synonym to 'diplomatic' is 'tactful', meaning considerate and sensitive. 'Official' may relate to being a diplomat, but is the wrong meaning for this context.

5 d bulky

The closest synonym to 'cumbersome' is 'bulky', meaning large and awkward to move. 'Tall' is incorrect because something could be tall but not awkward.

6 c article (The journalist wrote an **article** about a spate of burglaries in the area.)

'An' indicates that the missing word must be a noun beginning with a vowel, so only 'article' and 'extra' are options. 'Article' is the best answer as it means a piece written in a newspaper.

7 e dyed (Martha **dyed** her hair last week, but did not like the colour.)

The answer must be a past-tense verb since the sentence refers to 'last week', so 'colours' and 'dye' are incorrect. 'Died' and 'dead' are connected to 'die' rather than 'dye'.

8 d tested (Every Friday morning, the fire alarms were **tested**.)

All other options do not work with 'were' as the auxiliary verb.

9 b conferred (The quiz team **conferred** quietly about the answer before they wrote it down.)

'Conferred' means to have discussed something.

10 c unoccupied (The house had been **unoccupied** for five years.)

'Unoccupied' means not inhabited. 'Immobile' is incorrect as a house cannot move. 'Ruined', 'barren' and 'discarded' do not make sense in this context.

11 obligatory

'Obligatory', meaning compulsory, is the antonym for 'voluntary', meaning done from one's free will.

12 deliberate

'Deliberate', meaning done carefully, is the antonym for 'impulsive', meaning done without thinking.

13 polite

'Polite', meaning good-mannered and respectful, is the antonym for 'uncouth', meaning rude and ill-mannered.

14 biased

'Biased', meaning favouring one person or situation over another, is the antonym for 'fair', meaning considering both sides equally.

15 expose

'Expose', meaning to reveal, is the antonym for 'conceal', meaning to hide.

16 d role

In this sentence, 'capacity' means 'role' and is referring to the position of Mayor, not an amount of space (an alternate meaning of capacity).

17 a declared

In this sentence, 'pronounced' means 'declared' and is referring to the Mayor announcing the opening of the leisure complex.

18 d facility

In this sentence, 'complex' means 'facility' and is referring to the new buildings. It is not a synonym for 'complicated' in this context.

Test 2 (pages 6–7)

1 b fulfil (Dad decided to **fulfil** his lifetime ambition to run a marathon.)

The verb 'fulfil' is often used in connection with 'ambition' to mean doing something one has always wanted to do.

2 **e** ahead (Despite the rain, the race went **ahead**.)

The verb phrase 'to go ahead' is used to mean that something will be carried out. None of the other words make sense, although they may be connected to a race taking place.

3 **d** for (Emily had been learning to drive **for** a fortnight.)

The word 'for' is used here to denote a period of time, whereas 'since' denotes a point in time.

4 **a** at (The artist had a range of materials **at** his disposal.)

The expression 'at his disposal' means available to a person. The other options are incorrect.

5 **c** bus, **b** ail (The b**us**inesswoman checked her em**ail**s regularly.)

6 **d** act, **e** nit (The pr**act**ised every Wednesday in the commu**nit**y centre.)

7 **d** tea, **b** ram (Michael made a large **tea**r in his jeans when he sc**ram**bled over the gate.)

8 gue (fati**gue**, ton**gue**)

9 riz (ho**riz**on, p**riz**e)

10 ing (l**ing**er, **ing**enious)

11 qua (**qua**lify, e**qua**l)

12–16 The children **ate** their lunch contentedly, **looking** out of the windows and **thinking** of the mountains there **would** be to climb, the ponds, the streams to fish, the pictures to take, and the stories they **were** to hear all summer long.

Words not needed: eats, knew, stare, was

Test 3 (pages 8–9)

1 **e** our (With a fl**our**ish, the j**our**nalist left the room angrily.)

2 **c** bid (Anyone who did not a**bid**e by the rules was for**bid**den from taking part.)

3 **e** owe (I **owe**d him money for the fl**owe**rs.)

4 **b** fin (There was a staff brie**fin**g to discuss school **fin**ances.)

5 **d** can (The **can**didate had found the job va**can**cy advertised online.)

6 **b** pipe, **e** soaking

'Deluge', 'torrent' and 'downpour' are nouns referring to a large amount of falling water.

7 **c** noise, **d** silence

These words are both nouns. 'Peaceful', 'muted' and 'hushed' are adjectives and are synonyms for 'quiet'.

8 **b** carry, **c** kit

'Carry' is a verb and 'kit' is not a type of luggage, as 'satchel', 'bag' and 'briefcase' are.

9 **b** knew (Jamal **knew** he should have revised earlier.)

'Wished' is incorrect because it does not make sense with the modal verb 'should'. 'New' is the wrong homophone and 'know' and 'think' are the incorrect tense.

10 **e** on (She decided to go out **on** the spur of the moment.)

None of the other options is the correct preposition to use with 'spur of the moment', which is an idiom.

11 **d** practice (I went to football **practice** every Friday.)

'Practice' is the noun, whereas 'practise' is the verb. The other nouns need a determiner before the word 'football', such as 'a'.

12 **a** out (The weeds in the courtyard were **out** of control.)

Although 'under' can form a phrase with 'control', it cannot be followed by 'of'. None of the other words here make sense.

13 **d** despite (The dancer continued with the show **despite** hurting his ankle.)

Only 'despite' makes sense here when followed by the continuous form of the verb 'hurting'.

14 **b** rotten

The closest synonym to 'decayed' is 'rotten', meaning decomposed.

15 **e** absolve

The closest synonym to 'excuse' is 'absolve', meaning to forgive someone for something. Although 'excuse' can also be a noun meaning an apology (and pronounced slightly differently), there is no synonym for the noun 'excuse' here.

16 d lethargic

The closest synonym to 'listless' is 'lethargic', meaning having no energy or vigour.

Test 4 (pages 10–11)

1 vague

'Vague', meaning unclear, is the antonym for 'distinct', which means clear.

2 trivial

'Trivial', meaning unimportant, is the antonym for 'significant', which means important.

3 frugal

'Frugal', meaning simple and plain, is the antonym for 'luxurious', meaning extravagant.

4 chaotic

'Chaotic', which means disorderly, is the antonym for 'methodical', which means orderly.

5 worsen

'Worsen', meaning to make worse, is the antonym for 'improve', meaning to make better.

6 liberty

'Liberty', meaning freedom, is the antonym for 'imprisonment', which means being restricted.

7 c rse (The choir rehea**rse**d every Wednesday for the concert.)

8 a str (Carmel came second in the di**str**ict swimming competition.)

9 c oll (The driver had to swerve to avoid a c**oll**ision.)

10 daze (Being hit by a football left her in a **daze**.)

'Days' is incorrect as it refers to days of the week.

11 dense (The chocolate cake had a very **dense**, moist texture.)

'Dents' is incorrect because it means slight hollows in something.

12 eaves (The surveyor found woodworm in the **eaves** of the house.)

'Eves' is incorrect as it refers to a time of day.

13 healed (The cut on her foot **healed** quickly.)

'Heeled' is incorrect as this refers to a part of the foot or shoe (e.g. high-heeled shoes) and not the process of getting better.

14 waist (The trousers had a high **waist**.)

'Waste' is incorrect as this refers to things being thrown away.

15 d taut (The tightrope had to be **taut** in order to hold the acrobat.)

The word 'taut' means tight. 'Taught' is a homophone that refers to learning.

16 e recite (The children all had to learn a poem to **recite**.)

The word 'recite' means to perform something aloud. None of the other options makes sense.

17 a cue (The actor needed prompting when she missed her **cue**.)

Although there are other possible meanings, the word 'cue', in this context, means a sign to do something. 'Queue' is a homophone and refers to a line of people.

Test 5 (pages 12–13)

1 hurriedly

The synonym for 'quickly' is 'hurriedly', meaning fast.

2 sturdy

The synonym for 'robust' is 'sturdy', meaning solidly built.

3 restrain

The synonym for 'curb' is 'restrain', meaning to stop something or hold it back.

4 intrusive

The synonym for 'interfering' is 'intrusive', meaning nosy.

5 adversary

The synonym for 'rival' is 'adversary', meaning an enemy.

6 deflect

The synonym for 'divert' is 'deflect', meaning to make something change direction.

7–12 Jemima read through her lines one last time. She could hear the **orchestra** playing the overture and she knew that the **curtain** would rise at any moment. A tingle of nerves and **excitement** rushed through her body. After weeks of **rehearsals**, she knew she was ready. Hoping to give her best **performance** ever, she stepped onto the **stage**.

Words not needed: show, theatre

13 b retreat

The antonym of 'advance' is 'retreat'. 'Advance' means going forward, often used in connection with an army fighting a battle. 'Retreat' means to go back, often in the same context.

14 c safe

The antonym of 'risky' is 'safe'. 'Safely' and 'steadily' are incorrect as they are adverbs rather than adjectives.

15 e sharp

The antonym of 'blunt' is 'sharp'. 'Blunt' can also mean slightly rude and to the point. However, the only antonym given here is 'sharp'.

16 c worse

The antonym of 'better' is 'worse'. Both are comparative whereas 'worst' is superlative.

17 e different

The antonym of 'identical', meaning exactly the same, is 'different'. Both are adjectives, whereas 'difference' is a noun.

18 b orderly

The antonym of 'chaotic' is 'orderly'. 'Chaotic' means in disarray or disorganised. 'Tidily' is incorrect as it is an adverb.

19 sumptous, extravagant
20 peril, hazard
21 swift, abrupt
22 competition, contest

Test 6 (pages 14–15)

1 k bent, **m** twisted

These words are synonyms for 'crooked', meaning not straight.

2 b substantial, **i** immense

These words are synonyms for 'big', meaning large.

3 l affluent, **s** wealthy

These words are the opposite in meaning to 'poor', which means having little money.

4 h rude, **j** impudent

These words mean the opposite of 'polite', which means considering others thoughtfully.

5 d melancholy, **p** sorrow

These words are synonyms of 'sadness', meaning a feeling of unhappiness. 'Sad' is an adjective, whereas 'sadness', 'melancholy' and 'sorrow' are nouns.

6 b useful, **c** vital

'Needless', 'unnecessary' and 'pointless' are synonyms for something that has no use.

7 b placid, **d** lazy

'Rowdy', 'boisterous' and 'raucous' are synonyms for chaotic and noisy.

8 c tool, **d** fix

'Spanner', 'hammer' and 'screwdriver' are types of tools.

9 mane (As part of her stable duties, Gemma groomed the horse's **mane**.)

'Mane' refers to a horse's hair, whereas 'main' is incorrect as it refers to importance.

10 manner (The vintage uniform was embellished in an elaborate **manner**.)

'Manor' is incorrect as it means a large house.

11 air (A trip to the city made everyone appreciate the clean **air** of the countryside.)

'Heir' is incorrect as it refers to a person who inherits something.

12 herd (Driving down a country lane, Noel was forced to stop when a **herd** of cows crossed the road.)

'Herd' is the collective noun for a group of cows. 'Heard' is the past tense of the verb 'hear'.

13 vain (The nurse tried in **vain** to calm the patient down.)

'In vain' is an expression that means unsuccessfully. 'Vane' refers to a weather vane and 'vein' is a part of the body.

14 c spoke to

'Addressed' in this sentence means spoke to.

15 d notify

'Inform' in this sentence means notify. 'Betray' is incorrect as it is another meaning of 'inform'.

16 a forthcoming

'Imminent' describes something that is coming soon, so the correct answer is 'forthcoming'.

17 c brothers and sisters

'Siblings' means brothers and sisters.

Test 7 (pages 16–17)

1 **c** hat, **a** hot (Chris **hat**ed having his p**hot**o taken.)
2 **d** apt, **c** use (The audience burst into r**apt**urous appla**use** at the end of the show.)
3 **b** hum, **d** key (Jessica broke her **thum**b playing hoc**key**.)
4 **d** shy, **b** ear (The opera singer had grown a bu**shy** b**ear**d especially for the role.)
5 **c** van, **e** mat (Nadia sat the ad**van**ced **mat**hs exam.)
6 grate (Ashes from the fire fell into the **grate**.)
 'Grate' means part of a fireplace. 'Great' means good or large.
7 teeming (When she lifted the rock, the soil below was **teeming** with insects.)
 'Teeming' means swarming, whereas 'teaming' refers to forming a team with someone.
8 cellar (The **cellar** was full of new products ready for the market.)
 A 'cellar' is an underground room, whereas a 'seller' is someone who sells things.
9 horse (The Queen kept her **horse** on a very tight **rein**.) (2 marks)
 'Horse' is the animal, whereas 'hoarse' means having a rough voice. 'Rein' is a strap used to control a horse, 'reign' is the time a monarch rules and 'rain' refers to weather.
10 passed (As she **passed** the window, she noticed her friend inside.)
 'Passed' is the past tense of the verb 'pass', meaning to go by something. 'Past' also has the same meaning, but it is only used as an adverb, e.g. 'As she walked past the window, she noticed her friend inside'.

11–15 Sitting in her car in the traffic jam, Tiana suddenly **realised** that she knew the voice on the radio. It was her **former** English teacher, Mr Martin, who had taught her about Shakespeare many years ago. Now **here** he was, **presenting** a show about the plays. What a **surprise**!
 Words not used: hear, formal

16 indolent (lazy) – industrious (hard-working)
17 follow (to go after someone) – lead (to go before, to show the way)
18 frail (weak) – strong (having strength)
19 prohibit (forbid) – permit (allow)
20 undaunted (not put off) – discouraged (lost enthusiasm)
21 doubtful (unsure) – certain (sure)

Test 8 (pages 18–19)

1 **a** appreciate
 The closest synonym to 'savour' is 'appreciate', meaning to delight in something. Do not confuse with 'savoury', which is related to taste.
2 **c** confused
 The closest synonym to 'bemused' is 'confused'. None of the other words mean this.
3 **a** gloomy
 The closest synonym to 'dismal' is 'gloomy'. Both mean dreary. None of the other words mean this.
4 **b** extravagant
 The closest synonym to 'flamboyant' is 'extravagant', meaning very fancy or elaborate. None of the other words mean this.
5 **d** unclear
 The closest synonym to 'obscure' is 'unclear'. None of the other words mean this.
6 can (va**can**t, **can**cel)
7 pit (ca**pit**al, hos**pit**al)
8 air (ch**air**, **air**tight)
9 oil (sp**oil**t, t**oil**et)
10 ran (gua**ran**tee, frag**ran**ce)
11 for (in**for**mation, **for**bidden)
12 **e** outer, **f** exterior
 These words are antonyms for 'interior', which means inside.
13 **k** observer
 An observer watches but does not participate, like a 'fly on the wall'.
14 **h** coarse
 This word means the same as 'rough'. Do not confuse with 'course', which means a route.
15 **b** desert
 This word means to abandon someone. Do not confuse with 'dessert', meaning pudding.
16 **r** dessert
17 **g** fortunate, **n** fortuitous
 These words are synonyms for 'lucky', meaning having a good result.

Test 9 (pages 20–21)

1. **b** snail, **d** fox

   The other three words are all types of birds; these two belong to different animal groups.

2. **a** table, **c** plate

   The other three words are types of cutlery.

3. **d** reservoir, **e** pond

   The first three words are all types of naturally flowing water. The other two words are bodies of water.

4. **a** pear, **d** crop

   The other words are types of vegetables. 'Pear' is a fruit and 'crop' is a generic term for plants that are grown to be harvested.

5. **a** forest, **c** grow

   The other words are parts of a tree.

6. anxious

   The synonym for 'worried' is 'anxious', meaning nervous.

7. residence

   The synonym for 'dwelling' is 'residence', meaning a place where someone lives.

8. cunning

   The synonym for 'sly' is 'cunning', meaning devious or artful.

9. commence

   The synonym for 'begin' is 'commence', meaning to start something.

10. odour

    The synonym for 'smell' is 'odour', meaning an aroma.

11. **c** hope

    'Despair' means the absence of hope, so 'decline', 'ruin', 'worry' and 'contempt' are not opposites.

12. **e** rigid

    'Flexible' means bendy, so 'bendy' cannot be the antonym. Something that is rigid may be strong or robust, but neither is the antonym of 'flexible'. 'Capable' is also incorrect.

13. **a** lengthy

    'Brief' means short, so 'short' cannot be correct. The others are not antonyms of 'brief'.

14. **c** seldom

    'Often' means frequently so 'frequently' cannot be the antonym and neither can 'regularly'. 'Soon' and 'certainly' are also not antonyms.

15. **b** vague

    'Distinct' means clear or defined, so 'clear' cannot be the antonym. 'Special', 'pretty' and 'total' are also not antonyms.

16. **e** costly

    'Cheap' means inexpensive or economical, so 'economical' cannot be the antonym. 'Wealthy' is not an antonym, and neither 'money' nor 'poverty' are adjectives so could not be opposites.

17. At least (**At least** the weather had improved by the time the fair opened.)

    The phrase 'at least' here means if nothing else.

18. by no means (It was **by no means** certain that she would get a position on the football team.)

    The correct preposition to be used in this phrase is 'by', not 'in'.

19. under discussion (The exact arrangements for the forthcoming summer festival were still **under discussion**.)

    This phrase makes most sense in the context of the sentence as it implies that arrangements are being made for an event in the future.

20. in advance (The organisers offered a discount on tickets bought **in advance**.)

    The correct preposition to be used in this phrase is 'in', not 'on'.

21. out of the blue (Her long-lost cousin contacted her **out of the blue**.)

    'Out of the blue' is an idiom meaning without warning, which makes sense in this context. 'In the red' means in debt, which makes less sense here.

Test 10 (pages 22–23)

1. **c** r n q l (**tranquil**)
2. **b** e c l a (**peculiar**)
3. **d** a l a t (**valiant**)
4. **a** a t v e (in**active**)
5. prosperous (rich) – impoverished (poor)
6. vast (huge) – restricted (limited)
7. punctual (on time) – tardy (slow or late)

8   foe (an enemy) – ally (a friend)
9   humble (modest) – boastful (showing too much pride)
10 betrayal (letting someone down) – loyalty (giving support)
11 insert (put something in) – remove (take something out)
12 **d** prominent (The prize was donated by a **prominent** local businesswoman.)

    Prominent means well known and important. 'Preposterous' and 'probable' do not make sense. 'Amazing' and 'affluent' cannot follow 'a'.
13 **e** domestic (In Victorian times, wealthy families often employed **domestic** servants.)

    None of the other words make sense. 'Domestic' relates to the home.
14 **e** submit (Emil had to **submit** an application for the role of children's playleader.)

    'Submit an application' is a common expression when applying for a job.
15 **d** acquainted (The Grimshaw family invited their new neighbours in, to become better **acquainted**.)

    'Acquainted' means knowing someone.
16 **b** purpose (The safety inspector explained that the **purpose** of his visit was to check the play equipment.)

    'Purpose' here means reason.
17 generosity

    'Generosity' is the opposite of 'greed'.
18 flatter

    'Flatter' is the opposite of 'insult'.
19 abbreviate

    'Abbreviate' is the opposite of 'extend'.
20 cheerful

    'Cheerful' is the opposite of 'sullen'.

Test 11 (pages 24–25)

1   bit (am**bit**ion, **bit**ter)
2   ice (just**ice**, magnif**ice**nt)
3   our (harb**our**, fl**our**ish)
4   red (c**red**it, inspi**red**)
5   pen (ex**pen**sive, sus**pen**d)
6   and (c**and**idate, ab**and**on)
7   **e** fowl
8   **b** donate
9   **d** rarely
10 **c** happy, **e** naughty

    'Haughty', 'lofty' and 'disdainful' are all adjectives meaning arrogant or snobbish.
11 **a** jug, **d** water

    'Litre', 'pint' and 'gallon' all refer to units of measure for liquids.
12 **b** worried, **c** difficult

    'Conundrum', 'dilemma' and 'problem' are nouns referring to a difficult decision or worry.
13 **c** pass, **d** grow

    'Limit', 'restrict' and 'curb' mean to control or regulate something.
14–19 The **vessel** had been at sea for many weeks and the passengers on **board** were weary and **bored**. As the **harbour** finally came into sight, their **exhaustion** turned into **excitement** upon realising the opportunities ahead of them.

    Words not used: wave, luggage

Test 12 (pages 26–27)

1   ran (Maya's mum asked her to run an er**ran**d.)

    'Errand' means a short journey usually done to collect or deliver something.
2   sit (The couple paid a depo**sit** for their holiday.)

    A 'deposit' is a part payment made for a booking.
3   fit (It took two years for the business to make a pro**fit**.)

    'Profit' means money made from something.
4   mat, sum (The cook had to esti**mat**e how many meals would be con**sum**ed each week.)
    (2 marks)

    'Estimate' means to approximate and 'consumed' means eaten.
5   cup, our (Dad made sure he took plenty of games to oc**cup**y the children on their j**our**ney.)
    (2 marks)

    'Occupy' means to keep busy and 'journey' means a trip from one place to another.
6   **i** allow, **r** accept

These words are antonyms for 'refuse', meaning to not accept.

7 **e** solid, **f** full

These words are antonyms for 'hollow', meaning empty.

8 **b** conceited, **l** boastful

These words are antonyms for 'modest', meaning humble.

9 **c** free, **q** release

These words are antonyms for 'restrain', meaning to keep under control.

10 **k** wander, **o** roam

These words are synonyms for 'ramble', meaning to go for a walk.

11 **g** harsh, **m** stern

These words are synonyms for 'severe', meaning strict.

12 **b** submerge

'Immerse' and 'submerge' mean to cover in a liquid. This does not necessarily mean washing. It does not mean rubbing or painting.

13 **d** informed

'Informed' means 'notified'. Although the coastguard could have been 'telephoned', they could have been notified in another way. 'Prepared' and 'recorded' are also incorrect.

14 **d** in danger

The phrase 'in peril' means 'in danger'. This could involve being 'in the water' or being 'inexperienced', but it is not necessarily so. 'Informed' is also incorrect.

15 **c** tighten

In this context, 'contract' means 'tighten'. 'Expand' and 'relax' are antonyms of 'contract'. 'Promise' is a synonym of 'contract' when used with a different meaning.

16 **d** serious

The phrase 'in earnest' means serious. All other options are incorrect.

Test 13 (pages 28–29)

1–6 It was alien dress-up day at school and Josh had decided to wear the most **absurd** (or **peculiar**) costume he could make, in an **attempt** to **provoke** a reaction. He **refused** to listen to his mum when she told him how **peculiar** (or **absurd**) he looked dressed **entirely** in silver foil and metal coat hangers!

Words not used: restrained, moderate

7 smooth

'Smooth' is the synonym for 'sleek', meaning glossy or unruffled.

8 banish

'Banish' is the synonym for 'expel', meaning to make someone leave.

9 flourish

'Flourish' is the synonym for 'prosper', meaning to succeed, particularly financially.

10 barren

'Barren', meaning unable to produce something, is the antonym for 'fertile', meaning capable of producing something.

11 rare

'Rare', meaning not common, is the antonym for 'commonplace'.

12 divide

'Divide', meaning to separate, is the antonym for 'unite', meaning bring together.

13 **a** scarf, **e** glove

'Mackintosh', 'anorak' and 'overcoat' are all types of coat, whereas these two are not.

14 **c** fortnight, **e** day

'Millennium', 'decade' and 'century' are periods of time measured in years (1000 years, 10 years and 100 years).

15 **d** continue, **e** hurry

'Linger', 'loiter' and 'dawdle' are verbs that refer to staying somewhere longer than necessary.

16 **b** profit, **c** buy

'Merchant', 'trader' and 'dealer' are all nouns referring to a person who buys and sells things.

17 crowd, throng

18 ambition, aspiration

19 fecund, fertile

Test 14 (pages 30–31)

1 economical – prudent (cost-effective)

2 decline – deteriorate (to get worse)

3 trick – deceive (to fool someone)

4 quaint – whimsical (charming, unusual, fanciful)

5 entice – coax (to tempt someone)

6 condemn – denounce (renounce, put down)

7 to (All students were expected to conform **to** the uniform rules.)

8 of (In spite **of** the weather, they continued to climb to the summit.)

9 when (It is difficult to untie your shoelaces **when** your hands are cold.)

10 to (According **to** the website, the offer ended at midnight.)

11 on, of (The receptionist phoned Mrs Newton **on** behalf **of** the doctor.) (2 marks)

12 tip (mul**tip**le, **tip**toe)

13 art (**art**istic, dep**art**)

14 sum (as**sum**e, con**sum**er)

15 rib (des**crib**e, s**crib**ble)

16 **c** settle

'Resolve' means to settle a dispute or argument. Although this may involve punishing or supervising, this is not the actual definition.

17 **a** stop

'Cease' means to stop doing something.

18 **d** arms and legs

'Limbs' means both arms and legs in this context, so 'legs' only is not the answer.

19 **c** a teacher or coach

An instructor may read instructions and could be either a professional or a volunteer, but the main definition here is that an instructor is someone who teaches a specific skill.

Test 15 (pages 32–33)

1 **d** admit

'Deny' means to contradict or dispute something; 'admit' means the opposite. None of the other options are antonyms.

2 **c** destroy

'Restore' means to repair something; 'destroy' means the opposite. 'Build' is close in meaning to 'restore'. 'Broken' is an adjective rather than a verb. None of the other options are antonyms.

3 **e** diluted

'Concentrated' has a number of meanings, but the only meaning with an antonym here is 'diluted', meaning to have added a liquid to something to make it less strong. None of the other options are antonyms.

4 **b** tardy

'Prompt' means on time or quick; 'tardy' means late or slow to arrive. 'Punctual' and 'efficient' are close in meaning to 'prompt'. None of the other options are antonyms.

5 **e** flippant

'Sincere' means genuine, earnest or serious, so 'earnest' cannot be correct. 'Flippant' means thoughtless or not taking something seriously. None of the other options are antonyms.

6 arduous (hard-going) – effortless (easy to do)

7 benevolent (kind) – mean (unkind)

8 unkempt (untidy) – neat (tidy)

9 hygienic (clean) – unsanitary (dirty)

10 **b** arrogant, **e** mortal

'Modest', 'humble' and 'unassuming' all mean shy and unpretentious.

11 **b** angry, **d** curious

'Remorseful', 'repentant' and 'apologetic' all mean sorry.

12 **a** contempt, **d** shout

'Quarrel', 'dispute' and 'argument' are all words for a disagreement. Although this may involve shouting or contempt, they are not synonyms.

13 **a** signature, **b** article

'Promise', 'oath' and 'pledge' are all synonyms for 'vow'.

14 **b** avoid, **e** oppress

'Attempt', 'bid' and 'endeavour' are all synonyms, meaning to make an effort to do something.

15 g r e (**gar**ments)

16 c t t (**c**ons**t**an**t**)

17 e a t (**t**en**a**n**t**), a e n (**a**gr**ee**me**n**t) (2 marks)

18 e i e (**s**e**i**z**e**d), s s i (**pos**se**ssi**ons) (2 marks)

Test 16 (pages 34–35)

1 **b** b a d o (**a**ban**do**n)

2 **c** m m n t (co**mm**u**n**i**t**y)

3 **b** l p i a (di**l**a**pi**d**a**ted)

A9

4 **a** c s p c (**con**sp**ic**uous)

5 **d** n s n c (**nu**is**a**nce)

6 out of (It was **out of** the question to leave school early.)

7 on the (Sam was **on the** lookout for props to use in the pantomime.)

8 just in (They made it **just in** time for the concert.)

9 fed up with (She was **fed up with** her bossy sister.)

10 **e** obstinate

The closest synonym to 'stubborn' is 'obstinate', meaning strong-willed, although some of the other words may be used to describe someone who is obstinate or stubborn.

11 **c** extravagant

The closest synonym to 'ostentatious' is 'extravagant', meaning fancy or overly elaborate. 'Modest' is an antonym.

12 **d** baffled

The closest synonym to 'perplexed' is 'baffled', meaning puzzled or confused. Something that is 'complicated' may cause someone to be puzzled, but the two are not synonymous.

13 **d** scant

The closest synonym to 'meagre' is 'scant', meaning minimal. 'Generous' is an antonym.

14 **a** reprimand

The closest synonym to 'chastise' is 'reprimand', meaning to punish. 'Forgive' could be considered an antonym depending on the context.

15 sensor (The lights came on when the **sensor** was activated.)

A 'sensor' is a device that detects something, such as noise; 'censor' means to remove anything offensive from a text or film.

16 berths (They had booked a cabin with two **berths** on the cruise.)

'Berth' is a word for a bed on a ship, whereas 'birth' is when a baby is born.

17 marshal (It was the steward's job to **marshal** the spectators into the arena.)

'Marshal' means to organise people, whereas 'martial' means related to the military.

18 vein (The nurse struggled to find a **vein**.)

'Vein' is a part of the body that carries blood. 'Vane' is an instrument that measures wind. 'Vain' means proud of one's appearance.

19 ascent (She continued her **ascent** of the mountain despite the bad weather conditions.)

'Ascent' means to go up. 'Accent' is a particular way of pronouncing a language. 'Assent' means approval or agreement.

Test 17 (pages 36–37)

1–6 It was a hot summer's day and the family had decided to go on a trip to the countryside. Mum suggested they **avoid** the motorway so instead they took the **scenic** route. Soon, they left the town behind them and were driving on more **rural** roads. After an hour or so, they stopped to have a picnic. The cold cans of lemonade they had packed in the cool bag **quenched** their thirst. They had no **intention** of leaving the peace and **tranquillity** of the field for some time.

Words not needed: urban, saw

7 company

'The accountant had worked for the **company** for 20 years.' 'Company' in this context means a business.

'Priya wanted some **company** as she had been on her own all day.' 'Company' in this context means people to be with.

8 ground

'The criminal had obviously gone to **ground**.' 'Ground' in this context means gone into hiding.

'The **ground** was very slippery after the torrential rain.' 'Ground' in this context means the earth.

9 record

'Jeremy decided to **record** the new song he had written.' 'Record' in this context means to put down in a permanent way so that it can be referred to in the future.

'The Olympic medallist wanted to beat her previous **record**.' 'Record' in this context means a past achievement.

10 space

'They moved out of their flat because they needed more **space**.' 'Space' in this context means amount of room.

A10

'In the future, it may be possible to travel to **space**.' 'Space' in this context means the physical universe beyond Earth.

11   score

'Before baking the pie, the chef used a knife to **score** the top of the pastry.' 'Score' in this context means to partially cut.

'His highest **score** was over 200.' 'Score' in this context means a number of points.

12   **r** agile, **t** sprightly

These words are synonyms for 'nimble', meaning light in movement.

13   **b** gregarious, **p** companionable

These words are synonyms for 'sociable', meaning willing to talk and be involved with other people.

14   **c** abrupt, **q** offhand

These two words, meaning curt and impolite, are antonyms of 'courteous', meaning polite.

15   **i** omen

An omen is an event which is perceived to be a bad sign of things to come.

Test 18 (pages 38 and 59)

1   tier (He had tickets for the top **tier** of seats.)

'Tier' means a level or layer, whereas 'tear' is what comes from your eye when you cry.

2   complement (Mum chose a red scarf to **complement** her dress.)

'Complement' means to go with something, whereas 'compliment' is a nice remark.

3   stationary (They were warned not to get off until the train was **stationary**.)

'Stationery' refers to pens and paper (tip: think 'e' for envelope). 'Stationary' means not moving.

4   allowed (Mobile phones were not **allowed** in school.)

'Aloud' refers to sound, whereas 'allowed' means permitted.

5   site (The **site** of the new school was inspected regularly.)

'Sight' refers to the sense of seeing. 'Site' refers to an area of ground or a website.

6   yield – the amount of a crop produced

7   famine – a scarcity of food

8   pioneer – a person who is first to explore or discover something

9   idol – a person who is greatly admired or worshipped

10   pasture – land covered with grass

11   barren – land too poor to produce any vegetation

12   **b** deadly

The closest synonym to 'fatal' is 'deadly'. Although 'awful', 'harmful', 'dangerous' and 'flawed' may describe something that is fatal, only 'deadly' means 'causing death'.

13   **e** toil

'Toil' is another word for 'labour', meaning hard work. None of the other words are synonyms, although one might toil or labour with purpose or do so as a volunteer.

14   **d** permission

'Permission' is a synonym for 'consent'. None of the other words are synonyms.

15   **b** weak

'Weak' is a synonym for 'feeble', meaning without much strength. None of the other words are synonyms.

16   **a** merciful

'Merciful' is a synonym for 'lenient', meaning more forgiving than expected. None of the others are synonyms.

17   flimsy

'Flimsy', meaning easily damaged, is the antonym for 'robust', meaning sturdy or well made.

18   common

'Common', meaning frequently occurring, is the antonym for 'rare', meaning unusual or not frequently occurring.

19   corrupt

'Corrupt', meaning acting dishonestly, is the antonym for 'moral', which means acting in a way that is right or proper.

20   release

'Release', meaning to let go, is the antonym for 'capture', which means to take control.

Test 19 (pages 60–61)

1. for (uni**for**m, com**for**t)
2. cup (oc**cup**y, re**cup**erate)
3. end (**end**ure, att**end**)
4. out (**rout**ine, st**out**)
5. pan (com**pan**ion, **pan**tomime)
6. **c** bear, **e** wolf

   'Lion', 'panther' and 'leopard' are all types of big cat.
7. **b** bulb, **e** leaf

   'Daffodil', 'daisy' and 'tulip' are all flowers.
8. **a** support, **d** find

   'Keep', 'preserve' and 'cherish' are all synonyms for 'retain'.
9. **a** unusual, **e** lively

   'Monotonous', 'tedious' and 'boring' are all synonyms for 'dull'.
10. **c** family, **e** friend

    'Cousin', 'father' and 'niece' are all terms for different relatives.
11. **a** ally, **b** leader

    'Tyrant', 'oppressor' and 'dictator' all refer to a person who is a bully, often a political leader.
12. **c** admission, **d** promotion

    'Distress', 'anguish' and 'agony' all refer to extreme sorrow or pain.
13. sought (He **sought** her opinion on the film choice.)

    'Sought' is the past tense of the verb 'seek', whereas 'sort' means to organise or separate.
14. wring (After washing up, it is important to **wring** out the dishcloth.)

    'Wring' means to squeeze water out of something, whereas 'ring' refers to making a sound or circling something.
15. draught (Harry's grandad shut the curtains to keep out the **draught**.)

    'Draught' means a cool current of air, whereas 'draft' means a preliminary version of something, such as a piece of writing.
16. haul (The fishermen had to **haul** in their nets, which were full of fish.)

    'Haul' means to drag something heavy, whereas 'hall' is a type of room.
17. ceiling (The water had started to come through the **ceiling**.)

    'Ceiling' is the top of a room, whereas 'sealing' means fastening or closing up something securely.
18. **a** e i g e (re**sig**ned)
19. **c** u t t d (**cult**ivated)
20. **d** c m p o (**comp**osition)

Test 20 (pages 62–63)

1–10 Lola sat on the **stationary** train, holding her **railcard** in her hand. As the ticket inspector **approached**, she noticed the date on the top and **realised** it was **invalid**. She had **brought** the old one! Now she **risked** getting a fine. Could she **avoid** it? Only if the inspector **showed** her some **mercy**.

Words not used: stationery, bought

11. extract

    'The teacher read an **extract** from the book.' 'Extract' in this context means a short section from something larger, and is pronounced with emphasis on the first syllable.

    'The dentist explained that she needed to **extract** the man's rotten tooth.' 'Extract' in this context means to remove, and is pronounced with emphasis on the second syllable.

12. desert

    'Despite the arid heat in the daytime, a **desert** can be a very cold place at night.' 'Desert' in this context means a very dry region, and is pronounced with emphasis on the first syllable.

    'The traveller decided to **desert** his friend and return home.' 'Desert' in this context means to abandon, and is pronounced with emphasis on the second syllable.

13. **c** lean
14. **f** harbour
15. **d** score
16. **f** harbour
17. **c** lean
18. **d** score

    Words not needed: **b** cut and **e** thick

19. intermittent

    'Intermittent' means occurring at irregular intervals and is opposite to 'constant', meaning continuous.

20 disregard

'Disregard' means thoughtlessness and is opposite to 'consideration', meaning thoughtfulness.

21 untidy

'Untidy' means messy and is opposite to 'neat'.

22 lenient

'Lenient' means mild or having mercy and is opposite to 'stern', meaning strict.

Test 21 (pages 64–65)

1 **m** root, **t** source

These are synonyms for 'origin', meaning where something begins.

2 **b** rigid, **s** inflexible

These words are synonyms for 'unyielding', meaning unlikely to change one's opinion about something.

3 **a** disallow, **q** prohibit

These words are synonyms for 'forbid', meaning to not allow.

4 **c** revive

This word means to bring back to life.

5 **i** rank

This word means to put in order.

6 **g** minimum, **p** least

These words are antonyms for 'maximum', which means the greatest possible that can be attained.

7 **o** similarity

This word is an antonym for 'contrast', which means difference.

8 **b** crying, **e** happy

'Embarrassment', 'jealousy' and 'excitement' are all abstract nouns referring to feelings.

9 **b** lion, **d** elephant

'Gorilla', 'chimpanzee' and 'orangutan' are all types of primate, whereas the other two are not.

10 **a** car, **d** land

'Road', 'lane' and 'street' are all types of thoroughfare that cars drive along.

11 **b** finger, **e** stomach

'Calf', 'ankle' and 'knee' are all parts of the leg, whereas 'finger and 'stomach' are not.

12 **b** path, **e** garden

'Door', 'window' and 'porch' are all parts of a building.

13 **c** grow, **e** plant

'Wither', 'decay' and 'deteriorate' are all synonyms for 'decline'.

14 **e** promote (Ravi designed a poster to **promote** the festival.)

'Promote' means to advertise.

15 **c** adhere (Before using the computer suite, everyone had to agree to **adhere** to the rules.)

None of the other words make sense when followed by the word 'to'.

16 **b** employ (The film company needed to **employ** twenty people to work on the animation of the cartoon.)

17 **c** grate (The next step in the recipe was to **grate** the cheese.)

'Great' is a homophone of the correct word and means large or impressive.

18 **d** stoop (The doorway was so low, Dad needed to **stoop** to fit through it.)

'Stoop' means to bend one's head down.

Test 22 (pages 66–67)

1 **d** ventilation, **a** vapours (Good **ventilation** is needed to ensure the **vapours** from the dangerous chemicals can escape.)

2 **e** convey, **c** discontent (The residents staged a protest outside the council offices to **convey** their **discontent** with the plans to build a new factory in the area.)

3 **b** convince, **d** convert (The children hoped to **convince** their parents to **convert** the garage into a games room.)

4 **c** renowned, **e** temperate (The island was **renowned** for its **temperate** climate and beautiful landscape.)

5 end (ext**end**, indep**end**ent)

6 ran (ty**ran**t, er**ran**d)

7 men (gar**men**t, **men**tion)

8 tin (dis**tin**ct, ins**tin**ct)

9 den (impu**den**t, acci**den**t)

10 accept

'Accept' means to agree to something and is opposite to 'refuse', meaning stop or prevent something happening.

11 tardy

'Tardy' means late or slow to arrive and is opposite to 'prompt', meaning on time.

12 concede

'Concede' means to admit and is opposite to 'deny'.

13 contracted

'Contracted' means shortened and is opposite to 'extended'.

14 obstinate

'Obstinate' means awkward and is opposite to 'amenable'.

15 stadium – a place where sporting events are held

16 liberal – willing to accept opinions different to one's own

17 lecture – a presentation on a subject given by someone

18 lament – an expression of sadness or grief

19 methodical – done in an orderly fashion

20 companion – a person or animal who keeps one company

Test 23 (pages 68–69)

1 b c p t l (s**cept**ical)

'Dubious' and 'sceptical' mean unsure about something.

2 a b l g e (o**blige**)

'Compel' and 'oblige' mean to force someone to act.

3 d n l u s (co**nclus**ion)

'Ending' and 'conclusion' mean the finish of something.

4 d f f t n (af**fection**ate)

'Loving' and 'affectionate' mean showing fondness.

5 a c m r e (**com**p**re**hend)

'Understand' and 'comprehend' mean to recognise what something means.

6 e agitated

'Agitated' is opposite to 'tranquil'. 'Quiet' and 'calm' are synonyms. 'Special' and 'easy' are incorrect.

7 b occupied

'Occupied' is opposite to 'vacant'. 'Empty' is a synonym of 'vacant' and the others are incorrect.

8 c continue

'Continue' is opposite to 'halt'. 'Stop' is a synonym of 'halt' and the others are incorrect.

9 d flexible

'Flexible' is opposite to 'rigid'. All of the others are incorrect.

10–15 The children had been **begging** Mum to get a dog for as long as they could remember. She had always said it was too much **expense** and wouldn't entertain the idea. Finally, she had **conceded**, on the **condition** that they **adopted** one from the local dog rescue centre. From the moment they laid eyes on Bella the poodle in the centre, they were **devoted** to her forever.

Words not used: value, conclusion

16 flu, hoarse (Since having the **flu**, she had been very **hoarse**.)

'Flu' is an illness, whereas 'flew' is the past tense of the verb 'fly' and 'flue' is a ventilation hole for gases. 'Hoarse' means rough-sounding, whereas 'horse' is an animal. (2 marks)

17 wear, lessen (It is important to **wear** a cycling helmet, to **lessen** the impact in a crash.)

'Wear' is the verb referring to having something on one's body, whereas 'where' is in relation to position and 'we're' is short for 'we are'. 'Lessen' is a verb meaning to make less or reduce something, whereas 'lesson' is the noun referring to a period of teaching time. (2 marks)

18 knew, effect (No one **knew** what **effect** the medicine might have.)

'Knew' is the past tense of the verb 'know', whereas 'new' is an adjective referring to how old something is. 'Effect' is the change that happens, whereas 'affect' is a verb meaning to cause change to happen. (2 marks)

Test 24 (pages 70–71)

1 seam – a line where two pieces of fabric are sewn together

2 you – a pronoun referring to whom the person is speaking

3 taut – stretched or pulled tight

A14

4 seem – to give the impression
5 yew – a type of tree
6 ewe – a female sheep
7 **d** r i v t (**priv**a**t**e)
8 **c** s l n e (**silence**)
9 **e** a m n e (f**amine**)
10 **b** e x i r (**ex**te**ri**or)

11–18 After three years of trading, the **company** was starting to make a **profit**. Their bank account was finally in **credit** and they were barely keeping up with all the orders. The directors decided it was time to **employ** a new member of staff to be **responsible** for processing orders. They advertised the **vacancy** online and soon the applications came flooding in. After a day of tough interviews, they offered a **contract** to a young graduate called Sahil, who was the best **candidate** for the job.

Words not needed: agreement, companion

19 **b** common, **d** accustom

'Vague', 'obscure' and 'uncertain' are all synonyms meaning unclear.

20 **a** offhand, **d** rough

'Meaningful', 'significant' and 'serious' are words describing something that is important.

21 **c** old, **e** improve

'Deteriorate', 'worsen' and 'decline' all mean to get worse.

Test 25 (pages 72–73)

1 antidote

'Antidote' is a synonym for 'remedy', meaning a cure for something, particularly to reverse a poison.

2 honesty

'Honesty' is a synonym for 'candour', meaning openness.

3 effect

'Effect' is a synonym for 'influence'. Note that this is the noun, whereas 'affect' is a verb. 'Influence' can be either a noun or a verb.

4 remove

'Remove' is a synonym for 'extract', meaning to take out.

5 despise

'Despise' is a synonym for 'loathe', meaning to dislike intensely.

6 tradition

'Tradition' is a synonym for 'custom', meaning a widely accepted way of doing something.

7 **c** expensive, **d** private

'Economical', 'prudent' and 'frugal' all mean careful with money.

8 **b** special, **c** austere

'Fake', 'counterfeit' and 'hoax' all refer to something that pretends to be what it is not.

9 **a** partially, **b** evidently

'Wholly', 'completely' and 'entirely' all mean totally, or all of something.

10 **b** plunge, **c** insert

'Consume', 'ingest' and 'devour' all mean to eat something.

11 **c** proportion (The **proportion** of pupils with mobile phones has increased in recent years.)

'Proportion' is the best answer here as it means a number of something in relation to the whole.

12 **e** abode (The prince left his palace behind and took shelter in the woodcarver's humble **abode**.)

'Abode' is the best answer here as it means a place where a person lives. 'Habitat' is incorrect as it usually refers to the natural surroundings rather than the home itself.

13 **d** plume (Following the fire, a huge **plume** of smoke hung over the town.)

'Plume' means a long cloud of smoke. 'Clouds' is incorrect as the missing word must be singular, as shown by the article 'a'.

14 **b** lofty (From his **lofty** perch in the trees, the eagle surveyed the land below.)

'Lofty' is the best word here, as it means high up and the sentence clearly shows the eagle is high up, looking down on the land below.

15 **a** traitors (Guy Fawkes is one of Britain's most famous **traitors**.)

A traitor is someone who has betrayed someone or something, often their country. Guy Fawkes tried to blow up the Houses of Parliament.

16 c combination (The **combination** of too many sweets and a long car journey had made Sita feel ill!)

'Combination' is the correct answer here as the sentence shows there were two things making Sita feel unwell.

17 receipt (The cashier handed the customer a **receipt** for the purchase.)

18 dessert (After such a huge meal, we were all too full for **dessert**.)

19 contempt (The Queen looked at the greedy merchant with **contempt**.)

20 grown (The crop had **grown** tenfold by the end of the summer.)

Test 26 (pages 74–75)

1. **o** dedicate, **r** give

   These are synonyms for 'devote', meaning to spend a lot of time on or with.

2. **e** proclaim, **m** declare

   These are synonyms for 'exclaim', meaning to announce.

3. **b** job, **n** task

   These are synonyms for 'errand', meaning a task.

4. **i** persecute, **k** torment

   These are synonyms for 'oppress', meaning to cause distress.

5. **d** garment

   This word means an item of clothing.

6. **f** immortal

   This word means living forever.

7. **s** satin

   This word means a soft shiny fabric.

8. **a** unite, **p** combine

   These words are antonyms for 'detach', which means separate or divide.

9. sat (accu**sat**ion, **sat**ellite)
10. for (con**for**m, **for**tunate)
11. pit (hos**pit**able, ca**pit**al)
12. run (sh**run**ken, disg**run**tled)
13. pea (ap**pea**ling, **pea**ceful)
14. **c** conclusion (To finish her homework, Erin just needed to write the **conclusion** of her essay.)

The word 'finish' in the sentence implies that she is near the end, so the answer is unlikely to be 'extract' or 'preparation'. The others do not make sense.

15 e allies (During the Second World War, France and Britain worked together as **allies**.)

'Allies' is a word for countries that are on the same side in a war. Even if the historical context is not known, the clue is in the words 'worked together'. 'Foes' is its antonym.

16 d insolent (Following his **insolent** behaviour, the employee was sacked from the company.)

None of the other words make sense here.

17 e determine (They threw two dice to **determine** who should start the game.)

'Determine' can also mean 'decide'. The answer cannot be 'commence' because this would repeat the word 'start', which follows shortly afterwards. None of the others make sense.

Test 27 (pages 76–77)

1–6 The judge listened to all the **evidence** and **noted** the main points in the margin of his paperwork. Burglary was a very **grave** matter and he needed to ensure the punishment he gave was not too lenient. For that reason, he gave the criminal the **maximum** sentence **allowed**.

Words not needed: aloud, minimum

7. **c** weak

   'Weak' is most similar to 'infirm', meaning not physically or mentally strong. 'Healthy' and 'robust' are antonyms of 'infirm' and the others are incorrect

8. **d** strict

   'Strict' is most similar to 'stern', meaning serious and harsh. 'Strong' may imply a forceful character, but it is not a synonym for 'stern'.

9. **d** limited

   'Limited' is most similar to 'meagre', meaning scarce. All the others are incorrect.

10. **e** lunge

    'Lunge' is most similar to 'thrust', meaning to suddenly move the body forward.

11. resolve – to settle a problem
12. malady – an illness or disease

13 raiment – an old-fashioned word for clothing
14 coax – to persuade someone to do something
15 gratitude – thankfulness
16 caution – care taken to avoid mistakes
17 **b** p s e (op**pose**)
18 **d** c k s s (re**ckless**)
19 **c** e x l d (**ex**c**l**u**d**e)
20 **a** a c n t (**an**c**i**e**n**t)

Test 28 (pages 78–79)

1 **d** to accept (The director was pleased **to accept** the award on behalf of the whole cast.)

'Accept' here means to receive; 'except' is used to show that something is excluded. 'Too' means overly or to a higher degree, whereas 'to' is used in the infinitive form of a verb (e.g. I started to cry) or as a preposition (e.g. I ran to the shop).

2 **b** too idle (The boy was **too idle** to help his father with the housework.)

'Idol' means someone who is popular; 'idle' means lazy. 'Two' refers to the number, whereas 'too' means overly or to a higher degree. 'To' is used in the infinitive form of a verb or as a preposition.

3 **a** higher tier (The show was almost sold out and tickets in the **higher tier** were more expensive.)

'Higher' refers to height, while 'hire' means to borrow. 'Tier' refers to level, but 'tear' means the water from your eyes when you cry.

4 **c** their lapse (The accident was caused by **their lapse** in concentration.)

'Lapse' means a gap or error; a 'lap' refers to the flat area below the waist when a person sits, or a circuit on a racing track. 'Their' is possessive, whereas 'they're' is a contraction of 'they are' and 'there' refers to where something is.

5 **c** its site (The mine was filled in and a museum was built on **its site**.)

'Its' is already a possessive pronoun, so no apostrophe is needed. 'It's' is a contraction for 'it is'. 'Site' refers to a place where something is constructed; 'sight' refers to the act of seeing; 'cite' means to quote something.

6 current

'Current', meaning belonging in the present time, is the antonym for 'obsolete', meaning out of date or no longer used.

7 abundant

'Abundant', meaning plentiful, is the antonym for 'scarce', meaning in short supply.

8 satisfaction

'Satisfaction', meaning contentment, is the antonym for 'discontent', meaning a lack of contentment.

9 ambiguous

'Ambiguous', meaning imprecise, is the antonym for 'precise', meaning exact.

10 **c** origin, **e** pleasure

'Burden', 'hindrance' and 'hardship' all refer to something that is difficult.

11 **b** include, **c** offend

'Banish', 'ostracise' and 'oust' all mean to exclude someone and force them to leave.

12 **a** healthy, **d** temperate

'Wealthy', 'prosperous' and 'affluent' all describe being rich.

13 **b** garnish, **e** pollute

'Cleanse', 'sterilise' and 'scour' are all to do with cleaning.

14–19 The sound of **breaking** glass alerted the caretaker to the situation. Sure enough, there was a smashed **pane** in one of the sports hall windows. He knew immediately that it would **affect** lessons that day, so he foolishly tried to remove the worst shards of glass with his **bare** hands. Unfortunately, that resulted in his sustaining an injury that would **cause** him **pain** for a long time.

Words not needed: braking, effect, bear, course

Test 29 (pages 80–81)

1 secure – safe or unthreatened
2 wretched – extremely unhappy
3 destitute – extremely poor
4 despise – intensely dislike
5 complimentary – given free of charge
6 artful – clever in a cunning way

7 **b** lodge (The advert on television was misleading, so I decided to **lodge** a complaint.)

'Lodge' means to submit something.

8 **c** mere (It cost a **mere** five pounds to get a ticket.)

'Mere' means 'barely', or a small amount.

9 **d** worthy (The judge felt the cake was **worthy** of a prize in the competition.)

'Worthy' means deserving.

10 **e** occur (It did not **occur** to her that she should have brought a coat until it started to rain.)

'Occur' in this context means to realise something.

11 eat (thr**eat**en, cr**eat**ive)
12 act (distr**act**ion, subtr**act**ion)
13 one (pi**one**er, h**one**sty)
14 low (hol**low**, shal**low**)
15 tin (discon**tin**ue, ins**tin**ct)
16 **c** former

'Former' means old or previous and is opposite to 'latter', meaning most recent.

17 **b** adorned

'Adorned' is opposite to 'bare'. 'Empty' and 'meagre' are similar in meaning to 'bare'.

18 **e** approval

'Approval' is opposite to 'contempt'. 'Hatred' is a synonym. The other options are incorrect.

19 **c** candid

'Candid' means truthful or frank and is opposite to 'covert', meaning secretive. 'Secret' is a synonym. The other options are incorrect.

20 **b** inferior

'Inferior' is opposite to 'sublime', meaning of great excellence. 'Superb' and 'majestic' are synonyms. The other options are incorrect.

Test 30 (pages 82–83)

1 **a** kept back

The phrase 'in reserve' means 'kept back' in this sentence.

2 **b** a person with a long length of experience

Although 'veteran' can often mean an elderly person in a general sense, in this sentence it means a person with a long length of experience in a particular field.

3 **d** change the form of something

The word 'convert' means 'change the form of something' in this sentence.

4 **d** complaints

The closest meaning of the word 'objections' in this sentence is 'complaints'. Objections are often complaints that are opposing or refuting a particular idea.

5 **c** desire, **d** success

'Endeavour', 'attempt' and 'venture' all mean a try at doing something.

6 **a** fruitful, **d** flourishing

'Nutritious', 'wholesome' and 'nourishing' all mean healthy or good for you.

7 **b** roads, **d** traffic

'Village', 'town' and 'hamlet' are all different sizes of settlements.

8 **c** home, **d** outsider

'Resident', 'dweller' and 'inhabitant' all mean a person who lives in a place.

9 **a** sheep, **e** animal

'Swarm', 'flock' and 'pride' are all collective nouns for groups of animals (e.g. a swarm of bees, a flock of sheep, a pride of lions).

10 **a** loud, **d** sing

'Whisper', 'mutter' and 'mumble' are all synonyms for talking quietly.

11–19 Garrett Morgan was an American inventor who is famous for having **pioneered** an improved traffic-light **system**, as well as **designing** a gas mask, which was later **adopted** for use by the US army. His idea for improving traffic lights came about after he **witnessed** an accident **involving** a horse-drawn **carriage** and a car; he **realised** drivers needed a warning **signal** to stop.

Words not needed: inventor, cars

PUZZLE ANSWERS

Puzzle 1 (page 84)

Here are some suggested answers, but other answers that start with the correct letter are also acceptable. Check that your answers all match the categories.

A: alligator, accountant, apple, artichoke, apron, arm

B: bear, builder, bread, broccoli, boots, brain

D: dog, dancer, dates, dandelion, dress, diaphragm

J: jaguar, judge, jelly, juniper, jumper, jaw

P: panda, police officer, pickle, palm tree, poncho, pupil

R: rabbit, radiologist, rice, radish, raincoat, ribs

S: snake, surveyor, sandwich, sunflower, shirt, stomach

T: tiger, teacher, tomato, tulip, trousers, tongue

W: walrus, waiter, watermelon, willow, watch, waist

Puzzle 2 (page 85)

Start with checking the number of letters in each word. There is only one four-letter word (glad) and one six-letter word (joyous) so place these first.

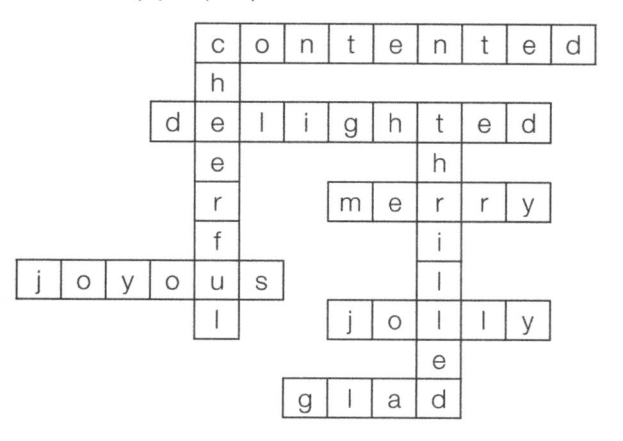

			c	o	n	t	e	n	t	e	d	
			h									
		d	e	l	i	g	h	t	e	d		
			e			h						
			r		m	e	r	r	y			
			f			i						
j	o	y	o	u	s							
			l			j	o	l	l	y		
						e						
					g	l	a	d				

Puzzle 3 (page 86)

Chain 1: deceit, tolerance, evil, luck, kindness, sorrow, wealth, happiness, strength, honesty

Only one word in the list can go in each of the spaces 3 to 5. The fifth word, 'kindness', ends in 's', so must be followed by either 'sorrow' or 'strength'. 'Honesty' must come last as it ends in 'y' and none of the words begins with 'y'.

Chain 2: amazement, tiredness, sadness, surprise, excitement, trust, truth, humour, romance, enthusiasm, motivation

For this chain, it is helpful to look first for the word that comes at the end: 'motivation', because it ends in 'n' and none of the other words begin with 'n'.

Puzzle 4 (page 87)

1. stream, brook, river (types of natural watercourse); pink, blue, green (colours); lion, tiger, puma (animals); lemon, lime, orange (citrus fruits); stool, chair, sofa (things to sit on)

2. holdall, suitcase, rucksack (types of bag); beach, bay, harbour (features found on the coast); beech, elm, oak (types of tree); hat, gloves, scarf (items of outdoor clothing); thyme, rosemary, mint (herbs)

3. bark, purr, growl (noises made by animals); midday, dawn, dusk (times of day); friend, collaborator, ally (synonyms for 'partner'); opponent, rival, foe (synonyms for 'enemy'); branch, trunk, roots (parts of a tree)

Puzzle 5 (page 88)

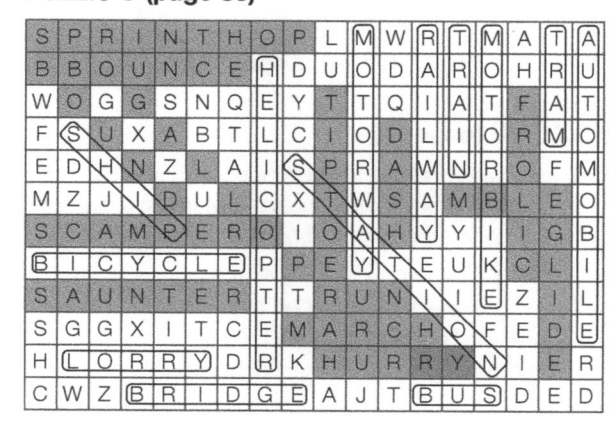

S	P	R	I	N	T	H	O	P	L	M	W	R	T	M	A	T	A
B	B	O	U	N	C	E	H	D	U	O	D	A	R	O	H	R	U
W	O	G	G	S	N	Q	E	Y	T	T	Q	I	A	T	F	A	T
F	S	U	X	A	B	T	L	C	I	O	D	L	I	O	R	M	O
E	D	H	N	Z	L	A	I	S	P	R	A	W	N	R	O	F	M
M	Z	J	D	U	L	C	X	T	W	S	A	M	B	L	E	O	
S	C	A	M	P	E	R	O	I	O	A	H	Y	Y	I	I	G	B
B	I	C	Y	C	L	E	P	P	E	Y	T	E	U	K	C	L	I
S	A	U	N	T	E	R	T	T	R	U	N	I	I	E	Z	I	
S	G	G	X	I	T	C	E	M	A	R	C	H	O	F	E	D	E
H	L	O	R	R	Y	D	R	K	H	U	R	R	Y	N	I	E	R
C	W	Z	B	R	I	D	G	E	A	J	T	B	U	S	D	E	D

Verbs of movement: dash, hurry, sprint, scamper, glide, saunter, amble, bounce, frolic, bound, run, tiptoe, march, gallop, hop

Words related to transport: train, automobile, helicopter, lorry, railway, motorway, station, ship, bridge, motorbike, bus, tram, bicycle

Puzzle 6 (page 89)

List 1: odd words out are sincere, irate (the others are synonyms for 'quiet')

List 2: trick, angry (the others are synonyms for 'disagreement')

List 3: snigger, furious (the others are synonyms for 'happiness')

List 4: chortle, candid (the others are synonyms for 'bendy')

List 5: prank, honest (the others are words meaning a point of view)

List 6: giggle, annoyed (the others are synonyms for 'stable' or 'tough')

List 7: truthful, fraud (the others are synonyms for 'deadly')

List 8: chuckle, hoax (the others are words meaning worn out)

Lists 9–12: sincere, candid, honest, truthful (words describing someone who tells the truth); irate, angry, furious, annoyed (synonyms for 'cross'); trick, prank, fraud, hoax (synonyms for 'deceit'); snigger, chortle, giggle, chuckle (synonyms for 'laugh')

Puzzle 7 (page 90)

Building: stable, flat, hut, shed, shop
Weather: rain, hail, snow, cloud, fog
Tree: ash, pine, oak, beech, lime
Colour: red, black, brown, orange, gold

Puzzle 8 (page 91)

1. micro: microwave, microscope, microphone; sun: sunstroke, sunflower, sunglasses; trans: transform, transport, transaction; fire: firefighter, fireproof, fireworks

2. super: supermarket, supernatural, superimpose; fore: forefinger, forehand, forehead; back: background, backfire, backache; snow: snowball, snowflake, snowstorm

When solving this kind of puzzle, think about common prefixes and also words that frequently make compound words. These are often nouns.

Puzzle 9 (page 92)

Modern: ancient, old, antiquated, obsolete
Big: minuscule, tiny, miniature, little
Happy: sad, miserable, melancholy, upset
Often: rarely, scarcely, seldom, hardly
Enemy: friend, ally, companion, buddy
Hot: cold, chilly, freezing, bitter

Puzzle 10 (page 93)

Here are some suggested answers, but other answers that start with the correct letter are also acceptable. Check that your answers all match the categories.

F: fish, flock, full, fix, faintly
G: gift, gaggle, generous, give, gallantly
H: head, herd, happy, hear, heartily
L: leg, litter, luxurious, lunge, loudly
M: mouse, murder, musical, make, magically
P: pipe, pride, perfect, plan, punctually
S: sock, swarm, small, seek, seldom
T: train, troop, tame, tremble, tastefully

Puzzle 11 (page 94)

jeans, genes; time, thyme; guessed, guest; whole, hole; eight, ate; censor, sensor; knight, night; air, heir; frays, phrase; phase, faze; birth, berth; urn, earn; meddle, medal; through, threw; sink, sync; marshal, martial; whale, wail

Test 18 continued from page 38

Select the **ONE** word on the right that has the most **SIMILAR** meaning to the word on the left. Underline the correct answer.

12 fatal   a awful   b deadly   c harmful   d dangerous   e flawed

13 labour   a purpose   b action   c contract   d volunteer   e toil

14 consent   a difficulty b concentration c disguise   d permission   e belief

15 feeble   a ghostly   b weak   c fake   d scarce   e sad

16 lenient   a merciful   b lazy   c short   d tilted   e spoilt

Find the missing letters that complete the word on the right so that it has an **OPPOSITE** meaning to the word on the left. Fill them in on the grid.

17 robust | f | | i | | | y |

18 rare | | o | | | o | |

19 moral | c | | | r | | t |

20 capture | | e | l | | s | |

> *Reading Tip!*
> Spellings, as well as word knowledge, are crucial for these questions. The best way to extend your vocabulary and spelling ability is to read a wide range of books, comics and magazines. You could even create your own spelling lists to learn, or make vocabulary flashcards.

Test 19

Find the missing three-letter word that completes both words. The same three letters are used for both words.

1 uni_____m   com_____t

2 oc_____y   re_____erate

3 _____ure   att_____

4 r_____ine   st_____

5 com_____ion   _____tomime

Select the **TWO** odd words out on each line. Select your answers by underlining **TWO** of the options **a–e**.

6   a lion   b panther   c bear   d leopard   e wolf

7   a daffodil b bulb   c daisy   d tulip   e leaf

8   a support   b keep   c preserve d find   e cherish

9   a unusual   b monotonous c tedious   d boring   e lively

10 a cousin   b father   c family   d niece   e friend

11 a ally   b leader   c tyrant   d oppressor   e dictator

12 a distress b anguish   c admission d promotion   e agony

Underline the correct word in each of these sentences. [5]

13 He (sought / sort) her opinion on the film choice.

14 After washing up, it is important to (ring / wring) out the dishcloth.

15 Harry's grandad shut the curtains to keep out the (draft / draught).

16 The fishermen had to (haul / hall) in their nets, which were full of fish.

17 The water had started to come through the (sealing / ceiling).

Find the missing letters that complete the word so that the sentence makes sense. Underline the correct answer from options **a–e**. [3]

18 The chef r __ s __ __ n __ d from her job.

    a eige   **b** egsd   **c** esge   **d** ersg   **e** eare

19 The gardener c __ l __ iva __ e __ the plants from seed.

    a ulte   **b** atte   **c** uttd   **d** lttd   **e** utdd

20 The musician gave a concert featuring a new __ o __ __ ositi __ n.

    a cnpo   **b** pmpo   **c** cmpa   **d** cmpo   **e** cmpi

> **Word Tip!**
> Sometimes it is difficult to find the missing letters just by focusing on the word itself. It can be easier if you read the whole sentence first to determine the context. What is it talking about? What words are associated with this context?

Total 20

Test 20

Read the following paragraph and add **ONE** word from the list to each space so that the paragraph makes sense. There are more words than there are spaces so some will be left out, but each word can only be used once.

> realised   approached   railcard   stationery   avoid   risked   mercy
> invalid   brought   bought   stationary   showed

1–10 Lola sat on the _____ train, holding her _____ in her hand. As the ticket inspector _____, she noticed the date on the top and _____ it was _____. She had _____ the old one! Now she _____ getting a fine. Could she _____ it? Only if the inspector _____ her some _____.

Each of the following pairs of sentences has a missing word. The same word can be used to complete both sentences, although the meaning is different. Write the word in the boxes.

11 The teacher read an _____ from the book.

The dentist explained that she needed to _____ the man's rotten tooth.

12 Despite the arid heat in the daytime, a _____ can be a very cold place at night.

The traveller decided to _____ his friend and return home.

Match each definition to a word from the box. Write the correct letter beside each definition. Some words can be used more than once. Not all the words in the box are needed.

13 to bend forwards _____

14 a place on the coast where ships moor _____

15 the number of points achieved by a team _____

16 to give shelter to _____

17 containing little fat _____

18 to scratch a line in a surface _____

a	compose
b	cut
c	lean
d	score
e	thick
f	harbour

Definitions Tip!
Remember that the same word can have more than one meaning and may not even be the same word class. For example, 'park' can be a noun and a verb.

Complete the word on the right so that it has the **OPPOSITE** meaning to the word on the left.

19 constant — i _ _ e r _ i t _ _ n t

20 consideration — d i _ r _ _ a r _

21 neat — _ n _ _ d _

22 stern — l _ n _ _ _ t

Test 21

Look at the words in the grid and then use them to answer the questions that follow.

a	disallow	b	rigid	c	revive	d	single	e	shuffle
f	credit	g	minimum	h	offensive	i	rank	j	big
k	mortal	l	plunge	m	root	n	largest	o	similarity
p	least	q	prohibit	r	difference	s	inflexible	t	source

1 Find **TWO** synonyms for 'origin'.

   _____   _____

2 Find **TWO** synonyms for 'unyielding'.

   _____   _____

3 Find **TWO** synonyms for 'forbid'.

   _____   _____

4 Find **ONE** word that means 'to bring back to life'.

   _____

5 Find **ONE** word that means 'to put in order'.

   _____

6 Find **TWO** antonyms for 'maximum'.

   _____   _____

7 Find **ONE** antonym for 'contrast'.

   _____

Select the **TWO** odd words out on each line. Select your answers by underlining **TWO** of the options **a–e**.

8   a embarrassment   b crying   c jealousy   d excitement   e happy

9   a gorilla   b lion   c chimpanzee   d elephant   e orangutan

10 a car   b road   c lane   d land   e street

11 a calf   b finger   c ankle   d knee   e stomach

12 a door   b path   c window   d porch   e garden

13 a wither   b decay   c grow   d deteriorate   e plant

The following sentences all have **ONE** word missing. Complete each sentence by selecting the **BEST** word from options **a–e**. Underline the correct answer.

14 Ravi designed a poster to _____ the festival.

   a propose   b prepare   c prompt   d prominent   e promote

15 Before using the computer suite, everyone had to agree to _____ to the rules.

   a follow   b obey   c adhere   d break   e accept

16 The film company needed to _____ twenty people to work on the animation of the cartoon.

   a entitle   b employ   c create   d agree   e extract

17 The next step in the recipe was to _____ the cheese.

   a great   b grade   c grate   d acquire   e accept

18 The doorway was so low, Dad needed to _____ to fit through it.

   a stool   b stand   c shrink   d stoop   e scant

Test 22

The following sentences all have **TWO** words missing. Complete each sentence by selecting the **BEST** words from options **a–f**. Write the words in the spaces.

1 Good _____ is needed to ensure the _____ from the dangerous chemicals can escape.

   a vapours   b air   c spill   d ventilation   e windows   f confine

2 The residents staged a protest outside the council offices to _____ their _____ with the plans to build a new factory in the area.

   a oblige   b petition   c discontent   d conduct   e convey   f offend

3 The children hoped to _____ their parents to _____ the garage into a games room.

   a contrive   b convince   c convey   d convert   e complex   f conflate

4 The island was _____ for its _____ climate and beautiful landscape.

   a received   b temperature   c renowned   d rumoured   e temperate
   f reserved

Find the missing three-letter word that completes these words. The same three letters are used for both words.

5 ext_____   indep_____ent

6 ty_____t   er_____d

7 gar_____t   _____tion

8 dis_____ct   ins_____ct

9 impu_____t   acci_____t

Complete the word on the right so that it has the most **OPPOSITE** meaning to the word on the left.

10 refuse | a | | c | | | |

11 prompt | t | | | | y |

12 deny | c | o | | | e | | e |

13 extended | c | o | | | r | | c | | e | d |

14 amenable | o | | | t | | n | a | | e |

Match each word on the left to its definition on the right by drawing a line.

15 stadium   an expression of sadness or grief

16 liberal   done in an orderly fashion

17 lecture   willing to accept opinions different to one's own

18 lament   a place where sporting events are held

19 methodical   a person or animal who keeps one company

20 companion   a presentation on a subject given by someone

Definitions Tip!
Read through the definitions and try to work out what kind of word it could be: a noun, a verb, an adjective and so on. Use suffixes to help you identify the word types in the given words on the left. For example, 'al' is often used at the end of adjectives, such as 'magical'.

Test 23

Find the missing letters that complete the word on the right so that it has a **SIMILAR** meaning to the word on the left. Underline the correct answer from options **a–e**.

1. dubious   s __ e __ __ ica __

    a k p u i   **b** c p t l   **c** k l p l   **d** h p t l   **e** c p k l

2. compel   o __ __ i __ __

    a b l g e   **b** b c l a   **c** c a b e   **d** b t e g   **e** b b l e

3. ending   co __ c __ __ __ ion

    a n c l s   **b** n l u t   **c** m c l s   **d** n l u s   **e** m k l u

4. loving   a __ __ e c __ i o __ ate

    a f f s n   **b** s s t n   **c** f t t m   **d** f f t n   **e** s c o t

5. understand   __ o __ p __ eh __ nd

    a c m r e   **b** c n p e   **c** r m o e   **d** s r h e   **e** c m p a

---

Select the **ONE** word on the right that has the most **OPPOSITE** meaning to the word on the left. Underline the correct answer.

6. tranquil   **a** quiet   **b** special   **c** calm   **d** easy   **e** agitated

7. vacant   **a** empty   **b** occupied   **c** confused   **d** silly   **e** convinced

8. halt   **a** stop   **b** high   **c** continue   **d** march   **e** rise

9. rigid   **a** tight   **b** solid   **c** pretty   **d** flexible   **e** strong

Read the following paragraph and add **ONE** word from the list to each space so that the paragraph makes sense. There are more words than there are spaces so some will be left out, but each word can only be used once.

> adopted   expense   condition   value   devoted   conclusion
> conceded   begging

10–15 The children had been _____ Mum to get a dog for as long as they could remember. She had always said it was too much _____ and wouldn't entertain the idea. Finally, she had _____, on the _____ that they _____ one from the local dog rescue centre.

From the moment they laid eyes on Bella the poodle in the centre, they were _____ to her forever.

Underline the correct words in each of these sentences.

16 Since having the (flew / flu / flue), she had been very (hoarse / horse).

17 It is important to (where / wear / we're) a cycling helmet, to (lessen / lesson) the impact in a crash.

18 No one (knew / new) what (affect / effect) the medicine might have.

Test 24

Match each word on the left to its definition on the right by drawing a line.

1 seam   stretched or pulled tight

2 you   a line where two pieces of fabric are sewn together

3 taut   to give the impression

4 seem   a female sheep

5 yew   a pronoun referring to whom the person is speaking

6 ewe   a type of tree

Find the missing letters that complete the word on the right so that it has an **OPPOSITE** meaning to the word on the left. Underline the correct answer from options **a–e**.

7 public   p __ __ __ a __ e

   a rive   b ravt   c rvte   d rivt   e rlte

8 din   __ i __ e __ c __

   a nsne   b sinc   c slne   d slnc   e quie

9 feast   f __ __ i __ __

   a anne   b amin   c amnn   d imne   e amne

10 interior   __ __ ter __ o __

   a xtro   b exir   c extr   d exor   e teor

Read the following paragraph and add **ONE** word from the list to each space so that the paragraph makes sense. There are more words than there are spaces so some will be left out, but each word can only be used once.

> agreement   candidate   company   credit   profit   employ
> responsible   vacancy   companion   contract

11–18 After three years of trading, the _____ was starting to make a _____. Their bank account was finally in _____ and they were barely keeping up with all the orders. The directors decided it was time to _____ a new member of staff to be _____ for processing orders. They advertised the _____ online and soon the applications came flooding in. After a day of tough interviews, they offered a _____ to a young graduate called Sahil, who was the best _____ for the job.

Select the **TWO** odd words out on each line. Select your answers by underlining **TWO** of the options **a–e**.

19 a vague   b common   c obscure   d accustom   e uncertain

20 a offhand   b meaningful   c significant   d rough   e serious

21 a deteriorate   b worsen   c old   d decline   e improve

Test 25

Complete the word on the right so that it has the most **SIMILAR** meaning to the word on the left.

1 remedy | a | | t | | | t | e |

2 candour | h | | | e | | | y |

3 influence | e | | | | | t |

4 extract | r | e | | | |

5 loathe | d | | s | | s | |

6 custom | | r | a | | t | i | | |

Select the **TWO** odd words out on each line. Select your answers by underlining **TWO** of the options **a–e**.

7 a economical   b prudent   c expensive   d private   e frugal

8 a fake   b special   c austere   d counterfeit e hoax

9 a partially   b evidently   c wholly   d completely   e entirely

10 a consume   b plunge   c insert   d ingest   e devour

The following sentences all have **ONE** word missing. Complete each sentence by selecting the **BEST** word from options **a–e**. Underline the correct answer.

11 The _____ of pupils with mobile phones has increased in recent years.

   a proposition **b** promotion **c** proportion **d** behaviour **e** conclusion

12 The prince left his palace behind and took shelter in the woodcarver's humble _____.

   a habitat **b** town **c** factory **d** castle **e** abode

13 Following the fire, a huge _____ of smoke hung over the town.

   a clouds **b** gas **c** fragment **d** plume **e** flourish

14 From his _____ perch in the trees, the eagle surveyed the land below.

   a vacant **b** lofty **c** lowly **d** feeble **e** wholly

15 Guy Fawkes is one of Britain's most famous _____.

   a traitors **b** idols **c** warriors **d** pioneers **e** candidates

16 The _____ of too many sweets and a long car journey had made Sita feel ill!

   a constellation **b** contribution **c** combination **d** temptation **e** objection

Underline the correct word in each of these sentences.

17 The cashier handed the customer a (receipt / recipe) for the purchase.

18 After such a huge meal, we were all too full for (desert / dessert).

19 The Queen looked at the greedy merchant with (contempt / content).

20 The crop had (grown / groan) tenfold by the end of the summer.

Time for a break! ★ *Go to Puzzle Page 92* →

Test 26

Look at the words in the grid and then use them to answer the questions that follow.

a	unite	b	job	c	voluntary	d	garment	e	proclaim
f	immortal	g	insert	h	boastful	i	persecute	j	whisper
k	torment	l	arrogant	m	declare	n	task	o	dedicate
p	combine	q	fatal	r	give	s	satin	t	sober

1 Find **TWO** synonyms for 'devote'.

_____   _____

2 Find **TWO** synonyms for 'exclaim'.

_____   _____

3 Find **TWO** synonyms for 'errand'.

_____   _____

4 Find **TWO** synonyms for 'oppress'.

_____   _____

5 Find **ONE** word that means 'an item of clothing'.

_____

6 Find **ONE** word that means 'living forever'.

_____

7 Find **ONE** word that means 'a soft shiny fabric'.

_____

8 Find **TWO** antonyms for 'detach'.

_____   _____

Find the missing three-letter word that completes these words. The same three letters are used for both words.

9   accu_____ion   _____ellite

10 con_____m   _____tunate

11 hos_____able   ca_____al

12 sh_____ken   disg_____tled

13 ap_____ling   _____ceful

The following sentences all have **ONE** word missing. Complete each sentence by selecting the **BEST** word from options **a–e**. Underline the correct answer.

14 To finish her homework, Erin just needed to write the _____ of her essay.

   a construction   **b** preparation   **c** conclusion   **d** caution   **e** extract

15 During the Second World War, France and Britain worked together as _____.

   a distance   **b** loyal   **c** traitors   **d** foes   **e** allies

16 Following his _____ behaviour, the employee was sacked from the company.

   a neat   **b** employ   **c** refuse   **d** insolent   **e** manners

17 They threw two dice to _____ who should start the game.

   a debate   **b** commence   **c** accustom   **d** acquire   **e** determine

Test 27

Read the following paragraph and add **ONE** word from the list to each space so that the paragraph makes sense. There are more words than there are spaces so some will be left out, but each word can only be used once.

> grave   allowed   minimum   noted   maximum
> aloud   evidence   lenient

1–6 The judge listened to all the _____ and _____ the main points in the margin of his paperwork. Burglary was a very _____ matter and he needed to ensure the punishment he gave was not too _____. For that reason, he gave the criminal the _____ sentence _____.

Select the **ONE** word on the right that has the most **SIMILAR** meaning to the word on the left. Underline the correct answer.

7 infirm   **a** loose   **b** healthy   **c** weak   **d** robust   **e** angry

8 stern   **a** helpful   **b** strong   **c** clever   **d** strict   **e** grumpy

9 meagre   **a** unkind   **b** menacing   **c** large   **d** limited   **e** absurd

10 thrust   **a** throw   **b** lose   **c** process   **d** spill   **e** lunge

Match each word on the left to its definition on the right by drawing a line.

11 resolve   care taken to avoid mistakes

12 malady   to settle a problem

13 raiment   an illness or disease

14 coax   thankfulness

15 gratitude   an old-fashioned word for clothing

16 caution   to persuade someone to do something

Find the missing letters that complete the word on the right so that it has the **OPPOSITE** meaning to the word on the left. Underline the correct answer from options **a–e**.

17 agree   op __ o __ __

  a pre   b pse   c ros   d psa   e pss

18 careful   r e __ __ l e __ __

  a csne   b cknc   c ckse   d ckss   e ksce

19 include   __ __ c __ u __ e

  a xtro   b exir   c exld   d elrd   e xldd

20 modern   __ n __ i e __ __

  a acnt   b apst   c enct   d asht   e asnt

Test 28

The following sentences all have a short phrase missing. Complete each sentence by underlining a phrase from options **a–d**.

1. The director was pleased _____ the award on behalf of the whole cast.

   a to except   **b** too accept   **c** too except   **d** to accept

2. The boy was _____ to help his father with the housework.

   a two idol   **b** too idle   **c** to idol   **d** two idle

3. The show was almost sold out and tickets in the _____ were more expensive.

   a higher tier   **b** hire tier   **c** higher tear   **d** hire tear

4. The accident was caused by _____ in concentration.

   a their laps   **b** they're lapse   **c** their lapse   **d** there laps

5. The mine was filled in and a museum was built on _____.

   a its sight   **b** it's site   **c** its site   **d** its cite

> **Two-Word Tip!**
> When selecting a short phrase, systematically check each of the two words. Once you have decided the correct first word, then look through to see which of the second words is correct.

Complete the word on the right so that it has the most **OPPOSITE** meaning to the word on the left.

6. obsolete   c _ r _ _ t

7. scarce   a _ _ n _ a n _

8 discontent | s | a | | i | | | a | | | i | o |

9 precise | a | | | i | g | | o | u |

Select the **TWO** odd words out on each line. Select your answers by underlining **TWO** of the options **a–e**.

10 **a** burden   **b** hindrance   **c** origin   **d** hardship   **e** pleasure

11 **a** banish   **b** include   **c** offend   **d** ostracise   **e** oust

12 **a** healthy   **b** wealthy   **c** prosperous **d** temperate   **e** affluent

13 **a** cleanse   **b** garnish   **c** sterilise   **d** scour   **e** pollute

Read the following paragraph and add **ONE** word from the list to each space so that the paragraph makes sense. There are more words than there are spaces so some will be left out, but each word can only be used once.

affect   braking   pain   bare   effect   pane   breaking   bear   cause   course

14–19 The sound of _____ glass alerted the caretaker to the situation. Sure enough, there was a smashed _____ in one of the sports hall windows. He knew immediately that it would _____ lessons that day, so he foolishly tried to remove the worst shards of glass with his _____ hands. Unfortunately, that resulted in his sustaining an injury that would _____ him _____ for a long time.

Test 29

Match each word on the left to its definition on the right by drawing a line.

1 secure   intensely dislike

2 wretched   safe or unthreatened

3 destitute   given free of charge

4 despise   extremely poor

5 complimentary   clever in a cunning way

6 artful   extremely unhappy

The following sentences all have **ONE** word missing. Complete each sentence by selecting the **BEST** word from options **a–e**. Underline the correct answer.

7 The advert on television was misleading, so I decided to _____ a complaint.

   a lead   **b** lodge   **c** complain   **d** deny   **e** appeal

8 It cost a _____ five pounds to get a ticket.

   a scarce   **b** only   **c** mere   **d** limited   **e** expensive

9 The judge felt the cake was _____ of a prize in the competition.

   a best   **b** given   **c** awarded   **d** worthy   **e** special

10 It did not _____ to her that she should have brought a coat until it started to rain.

   a realise   **b** idea   **c** procure   **d** occupy   **e** occur

Find the missing three-letter word that completes these words. The same three letters are used for both words.

11 thr_____en   cr_____ive

12 distr_____ion   subtr_____ion

13 pi_____er   h_____sty

14 hol_____   shal_____

15 discon_____ue   ins_____ct

Select the **ONE** word on the right that has the most **OPPOSITE** meaning to the word on the left. Underline the correct answer.

16 latter   a quieter   b special   c former   d prompt   e mere

17 bare   a empty   b adorned   c tight   d total   e meagre

18 contempt a hatred   b happiness c agree   d punish   e approval

19 covert   a worthy   b unwrapped c candid   d secret   e strong

20 sublime   a superb   b inferior   c majestic d friendly e amusing

Test 30

Read the following sentences and answer the questions. Underline the most sensible answer from options **a–d**.

'The veteran long-distance runner had some energy in reserve for the final lap.'

1   What does the phrase 'in reserve' mean in this sentence?

    a kept back   **b** used   **c** needed   **d** arranged

2   What does the word 'veteran' mean in this sentence?

    a an elderly person   **b** a person with a long length of experience
    c an extremely talented person   **d** an unpaid athlete

'The homeowner decided to convert the garage into a gym, despite numerous objections from the neighbours.'

3   What does the word 'convert' mean in this sentence?

    a score points   **b** knock down
    c persuade someone   **d** change the form of something

4   What does the word 'objections' mean in this sentence?

    a declarations   **b** suggestions   **c** good ideas   **d** complaints

> **Definitions Tip!**
> Try replacing the word in the sentence with each of the definitions to check if it makes sense in the context.

Select the **TWO** odd words out on each line. Select your answers by underlining **TWO** of the options **a–e**.

5   **a** endeavour   **b** attempt   **c** desire   **d** success   **e** venture

6   **a** fruitful   **b** nutritious   **c** wholesome   **d** flourishing **e** nourishing

7 a village   b roads   c town   d traffic   e hamlet

8 a resident   b dweller   c home   d outsider   e inhabitant

9 a sheep   b flock   c swarm   d pride   e animal

10 a loud   b whisper   c mutter   d sing   e mumble

Read the following paragraph and add **ONE** word from the list to each space so that the paragraph makes sense. There are more words than there are spaces so some will be left out, but each word can only be used once.

> realised   carriage   designing   inventor   involving   pioneered
> system   signal   cars   adopted   witnessed

11–19 Garrett Morgan was an American inventor who is famous for having _____ an improved traffic-light _____, as well as _____ a gas mask, which was later _____ for use by the US army. His idea for improving traffic lights came about after he _____ an accident _____ a horse-drawn _____ and a car; he _____ drivers needed a warning _____ to stop.

Puzzle 1

Alphabet Categories

Find a word for each of these categories that begins with the same letter given at the top of the grid. The first one has been done as an example.

CATEGORIES	A	B	D
Animal	alligator		
Occupation	accountant		
Food	apple		
Things that grow	artichoke		
Something you wear	apron		
Part of the body	arm		

CATEGORIES	J	P	R
Animal			
Occupation			
Food			
Things that grow			
Something you wear			
Part of the body			

CATEGORIES	S	T	W
Animal			
Occupation			
Food			
Things that grow			
Something you wear			
Part of the body			

Puzzle 2

Crossword

Can you fit the following words into the grid? They are all synonyms for the word 'happy'.

- contented
- delighted
- merry
- cheerful
- joyous
- jolly
- glad
- thrilled

I feel...

Puzzle 3 — Linking Letters

Put these words in order so that the last letter of one word is the same as the first letter of the following word. The first pair has been done for you. All of the words are abstract nouns.

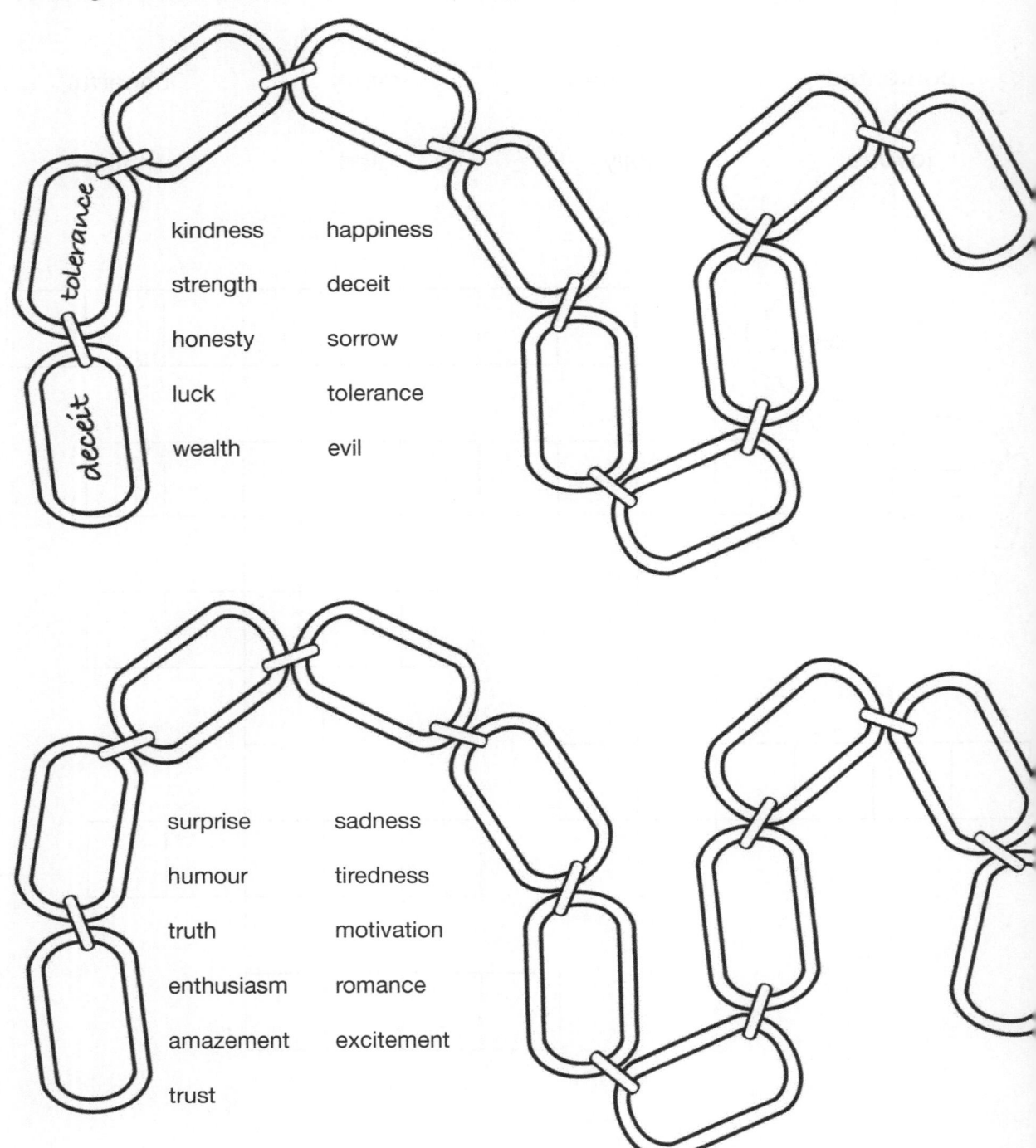

tolerance

deceit

kindness
strength
honesty
luck
wealth

happiness
deceit
sorrow
tolerance
evil

surprise
humour
truth
enthusiasm
amazement
trust

sadness
tiredness
motivation
romance
excitement

Puzzle 4 — Word Connections

In each 15-word grid below, there are five sets of words, each made up of three words that are connected. For each grid, find all five sets of three words – but be careful, as there are some words with more than one connection!

1

stream	lemon	stool	lion	brook
lime	tiger	pink	orange	chair
sofa	river	puma	blue	green

2

holdall	beech	elm	hat	thyme
gloves	beach	suitcase	bay	rosemary
mint	scarf	harbour	oak	rucksack

3

bark	friend	branch	midday	purr
dawn	opponent	collaborator	rival	trunk
ally	dusk	growl	roots	foe

Puzzle 5

Word Search

There are 28 words hidden in this word search. There are 15 verbs that refer to ways of moving. There are 13 nouns connected to transport. Once you have found them, write the verbs on the lines to the right and the transport nouns on the lines below.

```
S P R I N T H O P L M W R T M A T A
B B O U N C E H D U O D A R O H R U
W O G G S N Q E Y T T Q I A T F A T
F S U X A B T L C I O D L I O R M O
E D H N Z L A I S P R A W N R O F M
M Z J I D U L C X T W S A M B L E O
S C A M P E R O I O A H Y Y I I G B
B I C Y C L E P P E Y T E U K C L I
S A U N T E R T T R U N I I E Z I L
S G G X I T C E M A R C H O F E D E
H L O R R Y D R K H U R R Y N I E R
C W Z B R I D G E A J T B U S D E D
```

Puzzle 6

Odd Words Out

In each list of words, there are **TWO** words that do not fit with the other words. At the bottom of the page are four empty boxes and the odd words out, when sorted, make four lists with words that are connected. Find the odd words out and then place these words in the correct groups at the bottom of the page.

List 1
tranquil
calm
sincere
peaceful
irate

List 2
dispute
trick
argument
quarrel
angry

List 3
pleasure
joy
contentment
snigger
furious

List 4
flexible
chortle
supple
pliable
candid

List 5
opinion
viewpoint
prank
perspective
honest

List 6
strong
giggle
annoyed
sturdy
robust

List 7
mortal
truthful
fatal
lethal
fraud

List 8
exhausted
chuckle
weary
tired
hoax

List 9
_____
_____
_____
_____

List 10
_____
_____
_____
_____

List 11
_____
_____
_____
_____

List 12
_____
_____
_____
_____

Puzzle 7

Add or Remove

All of these words can have one letter added, or one letter removed, from any place in the word to make the name of a building, type of weather, type of tree or a colour. Add or remove the letter and write the new word on the line.

Building

table _____

fat _____

shut _____

she _____

hop _____

Colour

bred _____

back _____

brow _____

range _____

old _____

Weather

grain _____

ail _____

now _____

loud _____

frog _____

Tree

cash _____

pin _____

soak _____

breech _____

slime _____

Puzzle 8

Beginnings

For each of questions 1 and 2, there are four sets of three words. Each set of three words has the same prefix or compound word beginning (for example: **mis**take, **mis**lead, **miss**pelled; **head**band, **head**start, **head**room).

For each question set, find the prefix or compound word beginning that connects a set of three words. Write the prefix or word on the given lines.

1

_____wave

_____stroke

_____phone

_____fighter

_____glasses

_____port

_____flower

_____scope

_____proof

_____action

_____works

_____form

2

_____finger

_____storm

_____market

_____ground

_____hand

_____fire

_____head

_____ache

_____impose

_____ball

_____natural

_____flake

Puzzle 9

Anagrams

Unscramble these words. They are all opposite or almost opposite in meaning to the word given in the heading.

MODERN

t a n c n e i _____

d l o _____

q a e n u a t d t i _____

b o s t e l e o _____

BIG

s m u i u l c n e _____

n t y i _____

t i u m a r e n i _____

e t l l t i _____

HAPPY

a d s _____

b l e m r a i s e _____

l o c m a y h e l n _____

t u p s e _____

OFTEN

a r r y e l _____

e r s c l y c a _____

l o m d e s _____

d r h l a y _____

ENEMY

d r i e n f _____

y a l l _____

n a n p o m i o c _____

d y b u d _____

HOT

d o l c _____

l i c h l y _____

g r e f i n e z _____

b e r i t t _____

Puzzle 10 — Word Categories

Find a word for each of these categories that begins with the same letter given at the top of the grid. The first one has been done as an example.

CATEGORIES	C	F	G
Common noun	carpet		
Collective noun	colony		
Adjective	calm		
Verb	calling		
Adverb	coldly		

CATEGORIES	H	L	M
Common noun			
Collective noun			
Adjective			
Verb			
Adverb			

CATEGORIES	P	S	T
Common noun			
Collective noun			
Adjective			
Verb			
Adverb			

Puzzle 11

Homophone Hunt

Here are 34 words that make 17 pairs of **homophones**. Join each pair with a line.

- jeans
- time
- guessed
- whole
- eight
- censor
- knight
- air
- frays
- birth
- faze
- urn
- ate
- genes
- phase
- phrase
- heir
- hole
- guest
- meddle
- through
- berth
- earn
- medal
- sink
- marshal
- thyme
- night
- whale
- martial
- threw
- sensor
- sync
- wail

Key words

abstract noun A noun that denotes an idea, a quality or a feeling, rather than a concrete object, for example *happiness*.

antonym A word that means the opposite of another word, for example *hot* and *cold* are a pair of antonyms.

collective noun A noun used for a group of a particular thing. These are commonly used with groups of animals, such as *a swarm of bees*. Some animals have more than one correct collective noun.

connected words Many questions ask for connected words to be identified so that the 'odd word out' can be found. Remember to look for a connection to do with the following: a topic (for example *root*, *stem* and *leaf* are all connected as they are parts of a plant); the class of a word (for example *share*, *give* and *receive* are all connected as they are all verbs; watch out for verbs that can also be nouns, such as *walk*); synonyms and antonyms (for example *quiet*, *hush* and *peace* are all connected because they are antonyms of the word *noise*).

context Other words in a sentence help us to understand an individual word, for example the word *cut* may be used in two different contexts (as a noun or a verb). We need other words in the sentence to understand which meaning is being used: *I put a plaster on the cut on my finger* (noun). *Dad cut the wrapping paper with scissors* (verb).

definition A statement of the exact meaning of a word, especially in a dictionary, for example the definition of the word *noun* is *a part of speech that identifies a person, place, thing or idea*.

homograph A word that looks the same as another word when written, but has a different meaning. The words may also have different sounds when spoken, for example (1) *There was a tear in her eye*. (2) *The usher had to tear the ticket in half*.

homophone A word that sounds like another word but has a different meaning and may have a different spelling, for example *their, they're* and *there* are all homophones.

phrase A group of words that are grammatically connected, for example *The diver was equipped for the most inhospitable conditions*.

synonym A word that means the same as, or is similar to, another word, for example *small, tiny* and *little* are all synonyms.

vocabulary Words that are spoken, written and read. For example, we talk about having a *wide, extensive* or *broad vocabulary*, which means the number of words someone knows and understands.

word class Words that have the same function when used in a sentence, for example *nouns, verbs, adjectives, adverbs, prepositions, conjunctions*. These are also often referred to as 'parts of speech'.

Progress chart

How did you do? Fill in your score below and shade in the corresponding boxes to compare your progress across the different tests.

Test 1, *p4* Score: ____ /18	**Test 16**, *p34* Score: ____ /19
Test 2, *p6* Score: ____ /16	**Test 17**, *p36* Score: ____ /15
Test 3, *p8* Score: ____ /16	**Test 18**, *p38* Score: ____ /20
Test 4, *p10* Score: ____ /17	**Test 19**, *p60* Score: ____ /20
Test 5, *p12* Score: ____ /22	**Test 20**, *p62* Score: ____ /22
Test 6, *p14* Score: ____ /17	**Test 21**, *p64* Score: ____ /18
Test 7, *p16* Score: ____ /22	**Test 22**, *p66* Score: ____ /20
Test 8, *p18* Score: ____ /17	**Test 23**, *p68* Score: ____ /21
Test 9, *p20* Score: ____ /21	**Test 24**, *p70* Score: ____ /21
Test 10, *p22* Score: ____ /20	**Test 25**, *p72* Score: ____ /20
Test 11, *p24* Score: ____ /19	**Test 26**, *p74* Score: ____ /17
Test 12, *p26* Score: ____ /18	**Test 27**, *p76* Score: ____ /20
Test 13, *p28* Score: ____ /19	**Test 28**, *p78* Score: ____ /19
Test 14, *p30* Score: ____ /20	**Test 29**, *p80* Score: ____ /20
Test 15, *p32* Score: ____ /20	**Test 30**, *p82* Score: ____ /19